How to Housetrain Your Puppy

in 14 Days or Less

THE COMPLETE GUIDE TO

TRAINING YOUR DOG

Gretchen Pearson, DVM

HOW TO HOUSETRAIN YOUR PUPPY IN 14 DAYS OR LESS: THE COMPLETE GUIDE TO TRAINING YOUR DOG

Library of Congress Cataloging-in-Publication Data

Pearson, Gretchen.
  How to housetrain your puppy in 14 days or less : the complete guide to training your dog / by Gretchen Pearson.
    p. cm.
  Includes bibliographical references and index.
  ISBN-13: 978-1-60138-594-9 (alk. paper)
  ISBN-10: 1-60138-594-3 (alk. paper)
  1. Puppies--Training. 2. Dogs--Training. I. Title.
  SF431.P396 2010
  636.7'0887--dc22
                    2010037092

Printed in the United States

Printed on Recycled Paper

INTERIOR LAYOUT: Antoinette D'Amore • addesign@videotron.ca
COVER DESIGN: Jackie Miller • millerjackiej@gmail.com

A few years back we lost our beloved pet dog Bear, who was not only our best and dearest friend but also the "Vice President of Sunshine" here at Atlantic Publishing. He did not receive a salary but worked tirelessly 24 hours a day to please his parents.

Bear was a rescue dog who turned around and showered myself, my wife, Sherri, his grandparents Jean, Bob, and Nancy, and every person and animal he met (well, maybe not rabbits) with friendship and love. He made a lot of people smile every day.

We wanted you to know a portion of the profits of this book will be donated in Bear's memory to local animal shelters, parks, conservation organizations, and other individuals and nonprofit organizations in need of assistance.

– *Douglas & Sherri Brown*

PS: We have since adopted two more rescue dogs: first Scout, and the following year, Ginger. They were both mixed golden retrievers who needed a home.

Want to help animals and the world? Here are a dozen easy suggestions you and your family can implement today:

- *Adopt and rescue a pet from a local shelter.*
- *Support local and no-kill animal shelters.*
- *Plant a tree to honor someone you love.*
- *Be a developer — put up some birdhouses.*
- *Buy live, potted Christmas trees and replant them.*
- *Make sure you spend time with your animals each day.*
- *Save natural resources by recycling and buying recycled products.*
- *Drink tap water, or filter your own water at home.*
- *Whenever possible, limit your use of or do not use pesticides.*
- *If you eat seafood, make sustainable choices.*
- *Support your local farmers market.*
- *Get outside. Visit a park, volunteer, walk your dog, or ride your bike.*

Five years ago, Atlantic Publishing signed the Green Press Initiative. These guidelines promote environmentally friendly practices, such as using recycled stock and vegetable-based inks, avoiding waste, choosing energy-efficient resources, and promoting a no-pulping policy. We now use 100-percent recycled stock on all our books. The results: in one year, switching to post-consumer recycled stock saved 24 mature trees, 5,000 gallons of water, the equivalent of the total energy used for one home in a year, and the equivalent of the greenhouse gases from one car driven for a year.

Table of Contents

CHAPTER 2:
Canine Behavior..39

CHAPTER 3:
Safety Measures 45

Introduction

You have successfully completed the first step to housetraining your puppy — you picked up this book! This book will discuss different techniques used to housetrain your puppy, preparing the environment for your puppy, safety for your puppy, safety of the home from the puppy, what kind of behavior to expect from your companion, and how to troubleshoot any problem areas with your new companion. The main goal here is to accomplish this housetraining in 14 days or less. Although each of us is an individual, just like dogs, and each of us learns at our own pace, the guidelines in this book will help you and your puppy get on the same housetraining page in two weeks!

Provided within this book is a realistic timeline for completing the training process. You undoubtedly have heard stories about parents and the frustrations they faced while potty training their children — some taking years! If we keep these stories in the back of our minds, we will appreciate why potty training can be difficult at times, but the rewards are worth the work you put in.

Behavior is a vital part of housetraining and integral to owning a good citizen. Behavioral problems or lack of training are a leading cause of dog surrenders and ultimately, euthanasia. According to the American Association of Prevention of Cruelty to Animals (ASPCA), 5 to 8 million dogs and cats enter shelters each year, and 3 to 4 million of them are euthanized. This is a staggering and sobering number, but these numbers are actually down from figures of 15 years ago, when 15 to 20 million animals entered shelters, with 75 percent being euthanized.

House soiling was one of the most common reasons that owners surrendered their dogs to shelters, according to the National Council on Pet Population Study and Policy (**www.petpopulation. org**). Housetraining is a paramount factor in maintaining a long, pleasurable relationship between you and your pet. Consider this when you are helping your new family member learn and avoid being another one of these devastating statistics.

Spaying and neutering your pet has medical, overpopulation, and behavioral benefits for your pet. Unaltered male and female dogs will mark their territory. Spaying or neutering your pet will help prevent wandering and territorial marking and aggressive behaviors. This will also prevent unwanted breeding or pregnancy that further contributes to the pet overpopulation of our country today. False assumptions about spaying and neutering include thinking that a dog will be less protective of the home and his family or that a female should go through her first heat cycle before getting spayed or neutered. Ideally, for medical benefit and to prevent marking behavior, altering should be done by the time your dog is 6 months old.

Most puppies come to live with their new family after they are eight weeks old. Until then, it is important for a puppy to live with his or her mother and siblings to learn important social dog behavior. The first four months, or 16 weeks, of a puppy's life is a critical socialization period. All experiences they have, whether positive or negative, will greatly influence their outlook on the world and humans. This period will determine their levels of anxiety and fears and depth of human acceptance and bonding. A dog that does not have positive experiences, discipline, and proper guidance during this period may become overly fearful, protective, or withdrawn. The more positive the experiences they have, the easier it is for the dog to adjust to household life when growing up.

By nature, dogs are pack animals. They look to the alpha dog for leadership and direction. This leadership gives them confidence. Dogs are also clean by nature. They have one area that they rest, sleep, eat, and play, and a separate area in which they eliminate waste. When you understand these basic canine behaviors, you will be able to lead your dog and build confidence during the housetraining process and build a solid foundation for further training.

Even with a housetrained pet, problems and accidents can occur. To be on the safe side, you should first rule out medical conditions as the cause of these accidents. You can consult your veterinarian, dog trainer, book, and Internet sites to help you with housetraining tips and advice on ruling out medical conditions. *A list of these references can be found in the Appendix.* Once those are ruled out, you should be able to correct the problem. Here are a few examples of what can happen when medical issues are involved.

Kinsey, a 6-year-old Rat Terrier was a housetrained spayed female that, after a family split, went to live with her original owner. Kinsey's owner complained about her frequent urine accidents for the last couple of months. The owner thought these accidents were the result of the disruption in household dynamics and this was the dog's way of expressing that she was "mad at her."

When Kinsey went to live with her original owner, I examined her and performed a urinalysis to rule out any medical conditions. Kinsey was experiencing pain in her abdomen and lower back and would frequently cry out when picked up. Her urinalysis showed blood and crystals in her urine, so I did an x-ray to make sure she did not have any bladder stones. She did not, so I put her on pain relievers and antibiotics. At her age, a bladder tumor was also a concern, so I told her owner that if she did not respond to the medical therapy for a urinary tract infection and crystals, we would need to do an ultrasound and biopsy. It took several weeks of medication, as long-standing infections usually do, but today she is accident-free and much more comfortable.

This owner, who also happens to be my receptionist, had another female terrier that started urinating inappropriately in her home, and even on the owner's bed. We started with a urinalysis and blood work to rule out any underlying infection, kidney disease, or diabetes. The tests were all negative. I started her on a medication for hormonal incontinence, and she responded well initially. After a couple weeks, she relapsed, so I switched her to a syrup form of the medication. Now, she is accident-free.

Another client of mine adopted a 1-year-old spayed female Welsh corgi into her home, which already had another female corgi. This dog had a history of never being fully housetrained and had frequent accidents. The owners were diligent in trying to properly train her and gave her many opportunities to eliminate waste outside. Her urinalysis showed that she had a bacteria infection, so she was treated with antibiotics.

But, a couple of weeks after she went off her medication, she relapsed with more accidents and another infection. After working up her case with a urinalysis, blood work, x-rays, and an ultrasound, I discovered she had a very small defect in her bladder wall that was causing incomplete emptying of her bladder and a small pouch that allowed bacteria to breed in her bladder. Surgery corrected the small defect, and she has been accident-free since.

Dogs and humans coevolved 10 to 14,000 years ago, so our bond with these amazing creatures has a long history. Some owners think they must demand respect from their dogs, but if you neglect to return the respect, you will fail to earn the dog's trust. This is a critical point of developing the human-dog bond. Dogs are inherently pack animals and their relation-ships are based on a dominance hierarchy. By 4 to 5 weeks old, puppies already start to exhibit dominant behavior, biting and fighting amongst themselves. They are testing the strengths and weaknesses of their siblings as their first steps in establish-ing dominance and submission.

The leader of the pack maintains the bond of the pack. The lead-er will organize, dominate, and discipline the rest to keep or-der within the pack. Each dog knows his position in the pack, what members are above and below him or her in rank, and each knows his role. Dogs will seldom challenge a leader unless that leader becomes unsure, unclear, weak, or ill. It becomes very im-portant for your dog to establish this bond and respect with his "family pack."

You must establish rules as the pack leader and enforce them fairly, with a firm and loving attitude. Once you establish this leadership, you will always be in this role. If you do not take on this role, your dog will dominate you, be demanding and pushy, act inappropriately, and will be very difficult to train. Your dog will test all other animal and human members of the pack until finding his or her place.

Dog trainer Cherry Miloe, of Cherry's Corner offered this advice on why housetraining is so important:

"Giving dogs discipline is showing love for them. When they know the rules and what is expected of them, then they know the 'no' limit and can relax. What is expected of them must be clear. Otherwise, you will have a frantic dog, living in fear of you get-ting upset with them. Most dog training is very similar to rearing a child. Early childhood specialists will tell you that a child must know what to do and when to, or when not to, do the behavior."

Just as children will learn when and where they should properly go the bathroom, a puppy will also learn the appropriate place and time they should eliminate their waste.

This book will guide you through housetraining tips that are easy to follow and easy to understand. The goal is to provide you and the puppy a clean, safe home; to raise a canine that is a reliable, trustworthy companion and good citizen; and of course, to become another proud pet owner!

Basic obedience commands such as sit, down, stay, and come are the foundation of good behavior and will help you communicate focus to your puppy. You are on your way to the start of house-training your puppy with the "business-end" in sight and a short process that provide you with many happy years with your companion. So, it is time get started!

Ready, set, housetrain!

CHAPTER **1**

Are You Ready for the Puppy?

Most of you who have picked up this book likely have already adopted your new companion and want to start the process. Puppies take a lot of work and time, especially in the beginning. If your lifestyle requires your dog to be locked up for eight hours a day and you do not want to go outside often, or you cannot see yourself scooping poop, a dog may not be the perfect fit for you at this time.

The decision of bringing home a new pet requires you to be committed to the proper time it takes to train a well-behaved pet.

You must be present during this housetraining phase to be able to correct and to praise your dog every time it eliminates waste. You do not want to have a companion that you cannot trust or that you find to be more work than enjoyment — this is not fair to the puppy or to yourself.

Before you get the puppy, you should read and be familiar with what breed types most fit your personality, the traits of the dogs, and their exercise requirements. Dogs are social creatures that live in packs and do not like being left alone. Dogs will want to be close to you, in the house, and want to interact with their pack members and leader. Do not expect that you can get a dog and just put it in the backyard. Dogs that are chained or left alone for long periods will develop aggressive tendencies, become overly protective, and have a lot of pent up energy that may be difficult to control. If you have not yet adopted your puppy, you may want to answer some questions about your situation:

- "Is my family or am I ready to raise a puppy?"

- "Will my lifestyle and schedule allow me proper time and training for my puppy?"

- "What type of breed of dog best fits me and my family's lifestyle?"

- "How much will it cost me to raise a dog for 10 to 15 years?"

- "Am I ready to alter my schedule and provide a lifetime of care?"

These are big questions, and ideally you will have already considered their answers. On the other hand, the reward of this relationship with your new pet is an amazing experience of devotion and love. As Sigmund Freud explained, "Dogs provide affection without ambivalence, the simplicity of a life free from the almost unbearable conflicts of civilization, the beauty of an existence complete in itself."

The physical and mental environment of a puppy's new household should be stable and consistent and provide your puppy plenty of time to interact with you. If a household or its members are overly stressed by other commitments, they may have unreasonable expectations of their new puppy. The puppy will need guidance from a human member who is calm, assertive, gives clear instruction, and provides positive consistent leadership.

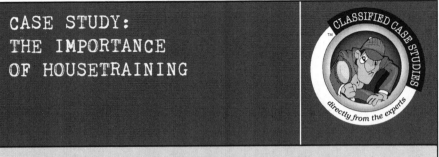

CASE STUDY:
THE IMPORTANCE
OF HOUSETRAINING

Dog trainer Juliet Whitfield of Durango Dogs, offered her professional opinion on the importance of housetraining:

If done properly, housetraining is the start of the communication process with the dog. If done quickly, it makes the owner happy. Housetraining takes as long as it takes; life often gets in the way; and people miss signals from their dog. Families, especially, often take months to train their puppy as they get busy with their hectic lives and can miss the signals.

The more you contain your dog and the more you can watch for the signals that your dog needs to go out, the faster the housetraining will go. The more time you can spend with your dog, the quicker it goes. The more distractions you have in your life, the longer it will take.

This process also grows longer if you allow your dog to roam freely in the house. Crate training is important if you cannot be with your dog 24 hours a day, which most of us cannot. If there is no crate, you must have a confinement room that is safe from all things that can be chewed. Housetraining goes very slowly for those humans who let the dog have the run of the house.

In addition, do not free feed your dog. Feed the dog distinct meals of a high-quality food that has meat as the first ingredient and no corn or wheat if possible. Pick up the food if it is not eaten at mealtime. Use some of the food for training and reward purposes. If the puppy has to be left alone, put food into toys that disperse food or require work to get the food, such as Kong® toys. If an owner has the resources, raw or cooked real meat diets and dehydrated mixes are recommended, such as produced by Honest Kitchen® or Sojos®.

Juliet's Tips for Housetraining Your Dog

- Your dog cannot be free in your house.

- All eyes must be on the dog at all times.

- Or tether your dog to you with a leash.

- Food = breakfast, lunch, and dinner. Food is down for 20 minutes, and then it is picked up if not eaten. No free feeding! This is to get your pup on a schedule.

- Create a schedule with your dog. Set a timer to remind you to take the dog outside.

- Pay close attention to your dog's body language. Does your puppy always start sniffing when he or she has to tinkle? Does he or she go to a certain spot? Be an eagle eye!

- You must go outside with your dog on leash every time he or she has to eliminate waste. Younger dogs if awake and playing might have to go out every 30 minutes to an hour.

- Your dog must urinate or have a bowel movement for you to go back inside the house. If you have run out of time, do the next best thing:

- If your dog does not eliminate outside, put him or her in a very small crate that he or she can stand in but barely turn around. If you use a bigger crate, your dog will eliminate waste in it.

- In five minutes, take your dog outside again. Repeat until your dog has eliminated.

- Use an enzymatic cleaner like Nature's Miracle® or Petastic®. Regular carpet cleaners will not remove the scent, and the dog will want to eliminate there again.

- Always take your dog out the same door to the same place to eliminate. This will create a routine for your dog.

- Give praise when the dog does eliminate outside. Be prepared with treats. Give your dog treats and praise immediately after eliminating waste.

You can contact Durango Dogs: Juliet Whitfield at 970-382-2542 or **info@durangodogs.com.**

Supplies You Will Need

Now that you have gotten a brief introduction to what you will face when housetraining your dog, you need to know what supplies will best help streamline this process.

The essential supplies to pick up before you bring your new puppy home:

- Collar

- Leash

- Crate

- Bedding

- Water and food bowls

- Enzymatic cleaner

- Paper towels

Choosing the collar and accessories

When choosing a collar for your dog, pick one that fits your dog comfortably and allows at least two fingers width between the neck and collar. The collar should not have excess items hanging from it or things that could fall off easily when the puppy scratches its neck. Characteristics of certain collars might appeal to your particular dog or you as the owner. Nylon collars are easy to clean. Rolled leather collars are good to prevent matting or tangling in long hair. Reflective collars are a nice option if you live in an area with a lot of traffic or tend to exercise your pet after dark.

Certain collars require a bit of precaution, though. Plastic collars are not recommended because they may stretch and break, and they contain petroleum products and odors that will be very close to the dog's head and face. Choker chains should not be left on the dog because they may catch on objects and strangle your dog if not closely observed. Prong or pinch collars are recommended only in the hands of professional trainers who know how to use them properly for correction of dogs that may be harder to train. These collars are used for correction and must not be left on the dog when he is not in active training times.

Head halters are nice alternatives for dogs that tend to pull excessively or for elderly or more petite people who may be at risk of being overpowered by their dog. The head halter is not a muzzle. It allows better control of the dog's head, like a halter on the horse. By controlling movement of the head, you control movement of the body without excessive force. The head halter fits over the top of the muzzle and fastens around the back of the head. The leash is attached to a ring underneath the muzzle, and the dog is controlled through the movement of the head.

Some breeds such as Bulldogs, Labrador Retrievers, and Arctic breeds such as Huskies, Samoyeds, and Malamutes have tremendous power and strength in pulling ability and can easily pull humans off their feet. It is important to teach your dog to walk nicely and calmly on a leash and not pull you. This becomes even more important in public areas around other humans and animals or on wet and icy surfaces. Harnesses encourage most dogs to pull against it with their strength and may make it difficult to control your dog. Harnesses are not recommended for training and should not be left on the dog other than when walking.

Identification tags with your name, address, and phone numbers are important in case of loss of your pet to aid in his or her return. Even if your pet lives in a fenced yard, it is still a good idea to always have ID tags on your dog in case of escape. Microchips can also be good permanent means of ID. A small chip, about the size of a rice grain, is implanted under the skin on the back of the net by your veterinarian or animal shelter. If your dog is lost, he or she may be scanned with a microchip reader that instantly identifies the owner. You must register this information and pay a small fee to the company. Make sure you keep your information updated to ensure prompt contact. Some companies also offer embroidered collars, which are a nice way to clearly see the information on the collar and avoid excess tags hanging from the collar that may be lost.

The right leash

A good leash is on your supply list, and you have two lengths to choose from. A short, four to six foot leash is good for walks out-

doors. A longer, 10 to 12 foot leash is good to train your puppy indoors initially and remain in control of his or her actions at "arms length," while still allowing some freedom to explore the environment. The longer leash is also good for "shy" dogs. It allows them to eliminate waste in their designated area without being under foot, allowing them some privacy at the longer distance. Retractable leashes allow a dog to explore at larger distances, but are difficult to control quickly, may tangle under you or your dog, and are not very strong for hard pulling or large breed dogs. Some dogs also may be frightened or intimidated by the sound of the recoil on the leash. The dog also may learn to keep constant tension on the leash while it pulls against it to get farther in front. The goal of leash walking is to have a dog heel by your side and walk with you nicely while maintaining slack in the leash.

A crate for sleeping and potty training

The sleeping and potty training tool of choice is the crate. This den space provides a safe quiet zone for your dog. *The size and types of crate appropriate for dog is discussed in Chapter 9.* You want to choose a solid, strong, easy-to-clean, safe, well-ventilated crate that your puppy can grow into.

Bedding material for the crate or home should be easy to launder, and special fitting pads can be bought for almost any size crate. Foam bedding is not necessarily recommended, especially for a puppy that may get bored or "diggers" who will quickly destroy the foam and turn it into popcorn. Very expensive foam bedding and orthopedic dog beds can be destroyed in a manner of minutes, even by the most innocent-looking dogs. Expensive bedding may look nice, but you should always be prepared for the fact that your little "angel" may indeed destroy it — your dog will have no concept or appreciation of the difference between a $5 blanket and a $150 bed!

A dish for feeding your dog

Food and water dishes come in a variety of sizes, material, colors, and weights. The dishes should be easy to clean and not contain any hazardous materials. Plastic bowls are not recommended because they may leach chemicals into the water; they are light-weight and easy for the puppy to chew; and they may cause sensitive reactions in the skin from constant contact. Ceramic bowls are heavier and tend not to slide when a dog is eating or drinking. They eventually will begin to accumulate mineral deposits from the water over time and can be more difficult to clean because they are somewhat porous. Stainless steel bowls come in a variety of sizes, are lightweight, and easy to clean and disinfect. Non-tip bowls are especially good for young puppies or overzealous eaters who tend to slide their bowls around. Stainless bowls have a wide base, often with rubber edging, which makes them very difficult for the dog to tip over and spill. Stainless steel buckets for water are designed to hang in the crate, off the ground, and prevent dogs from stepping or playing in their water dishes.

Cleaning supplies for your puppy

While training your puppy, you should be aware that accidents do happen. So, be prepared. Make sure you pick up enzymatic cleaner and paper towels to clean up after your new companion as he or she gets accustomed to the new environment.

Use an enzymatic cleaner like Nature's Miracle or Petastic. Regular carpet cleaners will not remove the scent, and the dog will want to eliminate there again.

Paper towels are self-explanatory, and you can never have enough in your arsenal. Always be ready to clean up after your puppy, and you should always keep your puppy's crate and living area clean.

Now that you have completed your supply checklist, you need to consider your schedule to adapt your lifestyle to your new companion and start training your puppy.

Considering Your Schedule

Now that you have a new member of the family, some important changes will occur when you bring home your new dog.

As you have already probably considered, your schedule needs to be altered to accommodate your new family member. If you are alone and are working outside the home, you will need to set aside time during the day to let your puppy outside to eliminate waste. This sounds simple, but timing is crucial to allow and reward the right thing happening. You may want to appeal for some help from your coworkers, friends, family, and neighbors. If you live with your family, engage all members in feeding, playing, and letting the puppy outside. It is important that you explain and carry out the schedule in order to be consistent and successful during the housetraining process.

For example, you let the puppy out of its crate and take outside at 7 a.m., then back inside to feed in the crate. While you are getting ready, the puppy can eat and play with its toys in the crate. At 7:20 a.m., you let the puppy out again to eliminate waste and allow some supervised outdoor play, exploration time, and exercise. You put the puppy back in the crate at 7:40 a.m. and leave for work, giving him or her another chance to eliminate outside immediately before you leave. At 11 a.m., you may leave for an early lunch break or have your neighbor come over to let the puppy out again. You may feed him or her again, too. At 2 p.m., perhaps your neighbor can come over again to let the puppy out, and at 5:15 p.m. when you get home, take the puppy outside again. As your puppy ages, he or she will be able to go for longer periods in the crate without having to eliminate waste, but it is important for the puppy not to eliminate in the crate. If family members are home all day with the puppy, you will have an opportunity to involve the whole family in this process.

Bringing home a new member to the family can be very disruptive to the whole household. New puppies will want to chew, chase the cat, play with the old dog, and play with you. Human members also will be affected, as a new family member requires a lot of monitoring and time. All members involved should stay on a feeding, playing, elimination, and sleeping schedule. Longtime pets may exhibit signs of aggression, jealousy, or even territorial marking behavior. Be sure to closely monitor your puppy at all times and step in when he or she begins to harass or could harm other members. This also will help the puppy understand that this new life is not a "free-for-all," and this household has rules. He is not in charge, you are. By establishing this "alpha" position of leadership and by maintaining a regular schedule, the puppy easily will learn what is expected of him or her.

You also want to keep in mind any pets that are currently part of your family. You must protect your other pets from the overzealous, excessive roughhousing puppy that may chase and hurt your other pets. This is especially notable for the geriatric dog that cannot tolerate a puppy jumping on its back or hips, knocking him over, or biting. You must not allow the puppy to chase the cats, the bird, or the pocket pets. The puppy may very easily injure or kill them in an instant with his strength or bite, even in play. The new dog also may affect the housetrained pet that you already have. They may begin territorial marking or inappropriate urination in presence of the new dog. Some cats disrupted in their routine may become anxious or upset and begin to eliminate inappropriately in their own home, such as on your bed, to express dismay with the situation.

All pets, just like people, are emotional creatures whose "feelings" must be taken into consideration during the transition phase. Your other pets will trust you as their leader when you protect them from the new arrival. Do not ignore the others and teach the new arrival rules of the home. Once your pets begin to see that this new member is staying and has a very distinct role in your pack, they will be more at ease and accepting of the situation.

One of the biggest mistakes new puppy owners make is paying enormous amounts of attention and lavishing praise to the puppy but tending to ignore their other dog or pets. This will cause jealousy, dislike, and reluctant acceptance of the newcomer. The new puppy should not be allowed to overrun the household and other pets or be allowed to do things, such as getting on the furniture, the other pets are not allowed to do. The pup-

py should be fed last, go through the door last, and bring up the rear in any other pet routines. This shows the puppy his or her order in the pack and does not disrupt the entire pack dynamic that has already been established in your house with your other pets. If you can remember these pack dynamics and how all your actions influence this dynamic, the transition and acceptance of your new dog will go much faster and smoother.

Considering Where To Get Your Puppy

Where your companion has come from can influence what he or she already knows and what still has to be learned. Obviously, an 8-week-old puppy is starting this process completely anew and

has relied on the mother to clean up after him or her, no matter where it went. If your pet is older or has come from a shelter or pet store, he or she may have been forced to eliminate in the sleeping area because he or she was not taken outside in a timely matter. Puppies in a pet store may know only paper or potty pads as a surface to eliminate on and perhaps never even touched the ground.

For example, a puppy was born at the clinic Elk Park Animal Hospital while his mother was being fostered. He and his nine other brother and sisters were born in the winter, and a lot of snow stayed on the ground for months. During his housetraining, he would seek out only the snow patches to eliminate on, and was somewhat perplexed when the snow began to melt. When he was taken to grassy areas to eliminate, he would hesitate to go, and it took an extra amount of encouragement for him to eliminate on this new surface.

Remember, just because you are outside, there are many different surfaces the puppy has to learn about — grass, dirt, mud, gravel, concrete, decking, and snow. This will require some retraining and relearning the correct elimination areas that you select. The techniques in this book can be applied to all ages and types of dogs.

Do You Have the Funds for a Puppy?

Many people who own pets are unprepared for the financial commitment that is necessary to raise them for many years. Consider that dog food averages $1 to $2 per pound and that a puppy may eat 35 pounds of food each month. Puppyhood vaccines average about $150. Then there is spaying and neutering, which can cost anywhere from $200 to $500. You also will have a lifetime of wellness and preventive care expenses, and perhaps unforeseen medical or surgical emergencies — a broken leg or foreign body removal, ranging anywhere from $600 to $2,000. Some dogs may live to be older than 15, and owning a pet is a lifetime of financial and emotional commitment that can reap a lifetime of reward in companionship.

The goal is to achieve housetraining in 14 days or less, but there will be daily opportunities for other training, experiences, learning, and bonding. Renowned Russian psychologist Dr. Ivan Pavlov and the "Pavlov" experiments showed that for a dog to commit a behavior to long-term memory, the dog must perform the task 42 days in succession, or 6 weeks. This book will follow the study of "shaping," or the practice of a positive reinforcement to effect some change in behavior, as presented by Harvard professor Dr. B.F. Skinner. American psychologist Dr. Evan Thorndike states that a behavior that results in a pleasant event (or reward) tends to be repeated, while a behavior that causes an unpleasant event tends not to be repeated. Positive reinforcement will be the hallmark of your training technique and can be followed in all further training for your puppy.

Basic supplies at hand and ready will simplify the process. Things you will need:

- Food and water bowls
- Collar and leash
- Baby gate(s)
- Pooper-scooper
- Plastic bags
- Dog bed or cushion
- Play toys
- Chew bone
- Grooming supplies: nail trimmer, brush, dog shampoo, ear cleaner, dog toothbrush
- Enzymatic cleaner and paper towels
- Rain jacket and footwear

CASE STUDY:
BEING PREPARED AND
OBSERVING THE PUPPY

Being prepared in all aspects of your personal and financial life is important to establish before bringing your new friend home. Dog trainer Cherry Miloe shares some of her experiences she had with her clients that resulted in financial and emotional stress caused by the inadequate preparation or observation of the puppy:

A 5-week-old puppy ate the leaves of a poisonous plant and went into convulsions. The vet was able to save him, but then, a week later, that same puppy jumped into a swimming pool and was under the cover of the pool. The vet resuscitated him again.

On another occasion, a neighbor had left a choke chain on the puppy, and when Cherry looked across the street, the puppy was caught on the cord of an outdoor blind and was choking itself. She ran over, jumped the fence, and released the puppy from its near-death experience. Because of that experience, she now uses cloth choker collars, only uses choker chains in training, and never leaves them on the dog.

CHAPTER 2

Canine Behavior

When you are deciding whether to get a puppy or how to approach housetraining your puppy, you need to understand the basic nature of canine behavior. Natural canine behavior exists in all our domesticated dogs but reflects ancestral roots of instinct. It is important to know what is just "natural" behavior for your dog and allow these behaviors to grow as your dog grows. Understanding canine behavior will help you be a more aware and educated pet owner. You are not raising a small human; you are raising a distinctive species much different than ourselves.

Social behavior

Dogs retain many of the behaviors of their ancestors, even though they are living in a modern world with humans. They live in small social groups; they follow a leader and show territorial

protection. They have a hierarchical social system that is relatively stable, and this structure helps prevent aggressive confrontations. Dogs use complex body language to exhibit dominant and submissive posture to maintain their social structure. In the domestic life of dogs living with their pack of humans, it is important that humans maintain the leadership role in the household.

Communication

Dogs use a variety of visual, olfactory, and vocal cues to communicate with each other. These cues help to transmit a variety of messages to other and from other dogs. These cues help the dog determine if a message is friendly or threatening. Vocalization can communicate caution with a growl or alerting with a bark. Dogs use their body language to communicate visual cues to other dogs. A dog may maximize his size to appear more threatening and protective, as a dog that curls up or rolls on its back indicates submission. Scent is a highly evolved sense in dogs that tells them a great deal about their environment and each other. Is it male or female? Is it receptive to breeding? Who was here last? What animals or humans have passed through here? Is it friend or foe?

Sexual behavior

An intact female dog exhibits through her hormones and body language that she is ready to receive a mate. A female dog has an estrus, or heat, cycle every six to seven months, beginning during her first year of life. In proestrus, the time before estrus, the female will become more social and playful and have increased frequency of urination. Intact male dogs also exhibit sexual behavior through the marking of territory, mounting, and roaming behavior. Spaying and neutering your pet will help eliminate or significantly curtail many of these undesirable behaviors.

Chewing

Dogs are natural chewers and will seek a variety of items to chew on. This helps release tension, curbs boredom, and helps keep their teeth clean. It is important to find the right toys that are not harmful when chewed or ingested and have a variety of texture or taste.

Aggression

Canine aggression is a common complaint of pet behavior and can have very serious or harmful results. Aggression is a threat or harmful action directed toward a group or individual. There are many reasons a dog may exhibit aggressive behavior, but aggression toward a human is dangerous and unacceptable.

Dominance aggression

Dogs use dominance aggression to gain and maintain a valuable resource, such as food, a bone, or a toy. This type of aggression may arise when a dog is disturbed when resting, is being led by the collar, is being groomed, or is being disciplined. The dog may exhibit body behavior such as a snarl, growl, direct stare, a high tail with quick stiff movement, or piloerection (hair standing). As a dog grows into maturity, this behavior may become more common between 1 to 3 years of age.

Fear aggression

Fear aggression is a behavior that dogs tend to show to other people, stimuli, or unfamiliar dogs. This fear may arise due to inadequate socialization, a genetic predisposition, or an adverse experience. This behavior may be exhibited toward men, children, an unfamiliar dog or noise, or the veterinarian. Often, these dogs may try to escape the situation before exhibiting aggressive behavior.

Predatory aggression

Dogs are natural-born hunters and chasers. Predation is an instinctual behavior and involves stalking, chasing, catching, biting, killing, and eating prey. This type of aggression is more prominent in certain breeds and can often be a very hard habit to break. These dogs may stalk and chase cats, children, birds, small pets, deer, or horses. Predatory aggression toward children or other pets is very dangerous or even fatal. This type of aggression can be very difficult to change and often carries a poor prognosis.

Territorial aggression

This type of aggression often occurs when a dog responds aggressively to unfamiliar animals or people that come into its territory. This can occur in the home, yard, or vehicle. These dogs try to appear larger by standing stiff-legged, ears and tail up, and with piloerection. They may also growl, bark, lunge, snap, and bite. This behavior usually develops after sexual maturity between 1 and 3 years of age. This type of dog, who always barks and lunges at the mail carrier, "wins" every time because he or she drove off the intruder (the mailman leaves). Remove these opportunities from the dog, and desensitize them by introducing a variety of visitors. The dog may be placed in social isolation for this behavior and needs to be adequately confined to prevent injury to people.

CHAPTER **3**

Safety Measures

Medical issues and disease prevention are a very important issue for your puppy. Medical problems can be inconvenient and even deadly to your cherished pet. Starting with a foundation of good health, it is imperative to your puppy's learning, growth, and success with training.

First, we shall discuss puppyhood vaccines. The most important of these preventable diseases is parvovirus. This virus in an unvaccinated puppy can cause explosive bloody diarrhea, profuse vomiting, dehydration, seizures, heart failure, and death. I have seen many young dogs die from parvovirus infection, and it is one of the most difficult diseases we treat as veterinarians. The real frustration and sadness comes from the fact that this disease could have been prevented with a simple series of vaccinations. A general puppyhood vaccine protocol is as follows:

First puppy package given at age 6 to 8 weeks:

- DAPPvCv
  (distemper, adenovirus, parvovirus, coronavirus)

- Deworming

Second puppy package given at age 9 to 11 weeks:

- DAPPvCv

- Bordetella (kennel cough vaccine)

- Deworming

Third puppy package given at age 12 to 16 weeks:

- DAPPvCv

- Bordetella

- Rabies

- Deworming

Your veterinarian may recommend a slightly different protocol or incorporate other vaccines that will protect your puppy from illnesses specific to your area or your dog's exposure. Deworming is also very important because your puppy especially is exposed to parasites and disease when exploring the environment with his or her nose and mouth. Piles of stool may contain many types of worm larvae and can survive some time outside in the stool or ground. A dog can become infected if he or she eats the feces or soil that is contaminated with worm larvae from other dogs. A dog can become infected with these larvae just by sniffing them, then licking its nose, and swallowing the larvae. Some parasites have zoonotic potential, or the ability to be transmitted from animal to humans.

Sanitation of the environment is important to prevent fecal to oral transmission from pets to children.

A Safe Environment for Your Puppy

Safety in your puppy's environment will provide you the peace of mind that your dog is safe when you leave him or her, and your home is safe from destruction. The "den" or crate space is a very useful tool in housetraining your pet. In nature, dogs look to sleep in a safe, confined, darkened, protected space in the form of a den. The crate mimics this natural instinct to seek out a den space. Crate training will significantly improve your housetraining effort, as most dogs will not eliminate waste in their "den" space. The crate has many advantages for you and your puppy.

A safety zone

Your dog cannot chew on items that may be harmful or things you do not want him or her to chew on, such as shoes and furniture. If your pet must be confined for health reasons, such as for the healing of a leg fracture or after a neuter, confinement will

be familiar and comfortable. The crate provides a place for you to put an overly exuberant puppy when guests or visitors arrive to prevent jumping on them. Crates are good for travel in the vehicle, on an airplane, or at a motel room and provide a familiar and safe zone for your puppy. And finally, the crate is a useful tool to allow you to leave your home and not worry about what surprises may await you when you get home.

What is a crate?

Crates are rectangular cages made of sturdy wire, molded plastic, canvas, or soft-sided strong fabric. Molded plastic crates are very strong and easy to clean. They are held together by nuts and bolts and come in a variety of colors. They are usually the least expensive way to maintain your dog's sleeping environment and most are suitable for airline travel requirements. Wire crates provide a good 360-degree view of the environment, often have two doors for easy access, and can fold up flat.

Wire crates have a more "open" feel and may not be appropriate for shyer or more reserved dogs that may feel intimidated by all the open space. Most wire crates can be covered with special fabric covers or just the top with a sheet or blanket. They have a removable tray in the bottom to make clean up easy.

Canvas crates are lightweight and can be folded easily for travel. Soft-sided crates are lightweight and are appropriate for small and toy-size breeds. They are best suited for travel, may have a shoulder strap or wheels, and can be suitable for carry-on luggage on the airlines. The crate should be large enough for your dog to stand up and turn around but not so large that he or she may want to eliminate waste at one end and sleep in the other.

Choose a crate your puppy can grow into. You may have to block off some of the interior if it is too large to begin with and remove the barrier as your puppy grows. Many different styles of crates are available, and they should be portable so you can travel with your dog's den. No matter where you go, he or she will always know where the safe spot is. Metal crates are prefered by some dog owners. They are durable, safe, portable (fold flat with a carrying handle) and can be covered more or less, as the environment dictates. Cover the crate with a sheet or blanket to darken the space, but make sure your dog can still see out and that the temperature is not too cold, too hot, and has adequate ventilation.

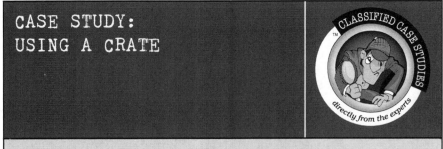

CASE STUDY:
USING A CRATE

Dog trainer Cherry Miloe discusses how she uses a crate in her home:

"I use a small crate for small puppies when they sleep or if I am going out for a little while. As they grow, so does their crate. I leave the door open and have toys in there, so they can go inside and take a nap or just rest. It then becomes their den where they feel secure. I crate puppies at night for at least the first year. I usually have another dog that they want to sleep next to at night, and I start letting them out, one night at a time, to see how they do. I do not want them to roam the house at night, so I put a gate across the door in the room in which they and the other dog are sleeping. My dogs usually sleep next to my bed, in their own beds. I still provide a crate for one of the dogs downstairs. It is the coolest and quietest place in the house, and she went downstairs every afternoon and took her nap there. She slept with a stuffed animal in there. I have a basket of stuffed animals and other toys that the dogs love to play with. I also keep a crate in the back of my van for puppies. In the crate, they are safe, have water, and toys, and I make sure they have plenty of air ventilation and park in the shade so they do not get too hot. I do not keep a blanket in with these young puppies, as they might get their feet, toenails, or teeth stuck in the fabric — I use a padded liner instead."

Choose one spot to place the crate — this will become your dog's home base. Because dogs are instinctually pack animals, they need to feel a part of the activity and be able to visualize the other members. Place the crate in an area that is not isolated from daily activities. Placing the crate in a corner of the living room is often a good area for your dog to observe what is going on with the family. A puppy that is isolated in another part of the house will often seek attention through excessive barking or trying to escape to be with its "pack." Your puppy will be integrated into the family much faster if he or she can see, observe, hear, and smell all the day's experiences.

Make sure to place the crate in an area that receives adequate ventilation, so fresh air can flow freely around it. The space must be a comfortable resting temperature and not placed in direct sunlight because this may cause your dog to overheat, especially in the summer. A warm environment is especially critical to young puppies that sleep alone because they would normally be resting with their mother or siblings and sharing in their body warmth. Ambient temperature for young dogs, less than 10 to 12 weeks old should be approximately 80 plus degrees. This can be accommodated with a warming sock or Snuggle Safe® that can be heated in the microwave to maintain its heat for many hours and is safer than a heating pad that puppies may chew on.

The crate space provides not only your puppy a safety zone but also your home. If you must leave the house for a period, you can securely put your puppy there and know there will be no chewing or destruction in your home. When you travel, the crate can be transported with you to new places, such as hotels or other friends' homes and gives the puppy a consistent familiar space. The crate gives you the control during housetraining to deter accidents and give you the ability to praise the puppy when you are there to praise the proper waste elimination. When you are home and able to supervise the puppy, let him or her out with the family to participate in daily events and play. The crate is a tool and not a convenience factor for inadequate supervision. Keep the crate door open when your puppy is out of the crate, so he or she always has access to the safety zone and resting place. You will find that your dog actually seeks it out when he or she wants to take a nap or even go into to it to play with toys. For aggressive chewers, appropriate chew toys may be Nylabone™ or Kong toys that are difficult to destroy. Hollow Kong toys allow you to place a food treat or peanut butter inside the hole to provide added interest and occupation for the puppy.

Fencing

Outdoor fencing is critical if you live in a busy neighborhood or if your pet has a tendency to wander. Many different fencing supplies are available, ranging from wooden privacy fence to mesh wire. The fence identifies an obvious boundary for waste elimination and protects your pet from escape or danger. Underground fencing also is available. The dog wears a collar that emits a warning or a shock when the dog approaches the fence boundary. Invisible Fence® and Pet Safe™ Boundary Control System are two manufacturers of these fencing systems. Regardless of the size of your dog's yard, always keep it clean and pick up fecal matter. This prevents contamination of children who may play there, odor and pest control, and curbs avoidance behavior when an area is soiled.

Dangers of Socializing Your Dog

Many people want to show off their newest family member to other dog-loving souls and will often take their puppies to public places, such as a park or dog park. This sounds like a good idea at first, but bear in mind the dangers you may unknowingly expose your puppy to.

Parks are areas where many unknown dogs with unknown vaccine histories have been. This exposes your puppy to diseases, such as parvovirus, which may exist in the environment for five years, unaffected by sunshine or freezing. What you do not know (or see) may hurt your puppy. Socialization is an invaluable tool for all dogs, but be cautious about your choice of environment and the age of your dog. Puppies younger than four months are most at risk because their immune systems are not fully mature. This is why it is so important to protect your puppy with puppyhood vaccinations to build their immunity to this devastating disease. Make sure that whoever handles your puppy has not already handled other infected or carrier dogs, or that other dogs your puppy contacts are healthy. Do not feel panicked or threatened, just informed about who and what touches your puppy.

Dangers at Home

The home environment may contain many items that could harm our puppies — light sockets, lamps, shoes, household cleaners, jewelry, pencils, paper clips, loose change, swimming pools, trash cans, toilets, plastic, choking hazards, bags, and plants. Try to remove everything within eye-level of a puppy to prevent obvious destruction or accidents. You should be aware of many common house and yard plants that can be toxic to your pet:

TOXIC HOUSEPLANTS		
Aloe vera	Dumbcane	Rubber plant
Asparagus fern	Lilies	Umbrella plant
Cactus	Mistletoe	Various ivies
Caladium	Philodendron	
Chrysanthemum	Poinsettia	

TOXIC OUTDOOR PLANTS		
Autumn crocus	Jerusalem cherry	Oleander
Castor bean	Kalanchoe	Precatory beans
Foxglove	Larkspur	Trumpet vine
Hibiscus	Lily of the valley	Tulips
Hyacinth	Morning glory	Wisteria
Japanese yew	Nightshade	

CHAPTER **4**

Preparing the Environment

When preparing your puppy's environment, first gather the proper materials you will need to housetrain your puppy. Have a collar and leash to be able to take him or her outside. A long (20 feet) leash allows the puppy to explore the elimination spot but still gives you control if he or she starts to stray. Have a roll of paper towels and odor neutralizer on hand to make cleanups fast and easy. A covered trashcan keeps cleanup odors to a minimum. Prepare an easy pair of shoes to slip on and a jacket near the doorway. A towel will be useful to wipe off wet or muddy paws when returning inside. You will want to have your chosen crate assembled and ready and baby gates to safely block off areas that you do not want your puppy to reach.

It is a good idea to track your puppy's waste elimination times to help you visualize his or her timing and make adjustments to your schedule. Make sure the spaces where your puppy will sleep and play do not contain any hazards. Remove toxic plants, electrical cords and children's toys from the area and "puppy-proof" your living space to prevent unwanted chewing disasters. In the previous chapter, we touched upon the importance of the den space or crate. Using the crate will help speed up the process of housetraining because a dog does not wish to eliminate where he or she sleeps or eats. This is good news for you and enforces a place of safety, security, and cleanliness and not a site to eliminate in. The crate helps you provide a safety zone for your puppy to sleep and eat, and it provides a place of mindful and body rest. Anxious, shy, or unsure dogs really need this den to feel safe from the world or to retreat to when they are unsure of the situation at hand. If you are introducing a puppy to a crate for the first time after it has been used to a life of "freedom without borders," you may experience some resistance to the idea. But fear not, stay true to your belief that the den is a good space, and do not give in to the barking or whining that may ensue. Most puppies adapt to their crate within days. Just like any good parent, your children may want to eat all the cookies in the jar, but you know what is best for them. If you do not think the crate is someplace you will want your dog sleeping all of its life, that is OK, but remember it will give you better control of the environment and your puppy during the housetraining process. If you work outside of the home, your pet will be in a place that it cannot get into the trash, chew on the couch, chase the cat, or leave you unwanted surprises at the end of the day. Adult dogs may be crated up to eight hours without accidents but ideally would be allowed out to exercise and play. Young puppies that are 6 to 8 weeks old need to go out every one to two hours.

Where you put the crate is another factor in how well it is accepted by your dog. We already discussed proper temperature and ventilation, but visualization is important, too. Even if your dog is in the den, he or she still needs to feel amongst the "pack." Dogs are social, pack behavior animals and need to be able to see what is happening in their environment to feel at ease. You would not want to be locked up in the basement or the bathroom, and neither will they. Instead, choose a quiet corner of the living room where they may still be part of the activity, even when they are in their den.

The space needs to be private but not isolated, quiet but not silent, clean, and odor-free.

Do not use the crate as punishment, isolation, or for extended periods of "lockdown." You want your dog to always feel secure and provide a shelter of comfort and security as a good place to be.

If your puppy has not been crate-trained, he or she may at first object to being subjected to a restricted space. He or she may bark, whine, or paw at the door. Do not give in to these objections from your puppy and let him or her out of the crate. Only do so when the puppy is quiet, calm, and behaving. Usually this temper tantrum may last only a couple days, and your puppy will quickly learn that misbehaving will not give it what it wants. Do not reassure or say, "it is OK" or "good boy" when the puppy is misbehaving because this will only provide encouragement that the behavior is acceptable or rewarded by you. This is another new lesson in the learning process that life has rules and rewards, and roaming is not allowed. Good behavior is expected to get praise from you. There are defined spaces and times for feeding, sleeping, and playing. Once your puppy begins to understand these new rules, the occasional whine or bark is acceptable when he or she needs to go out.

Providing toys in the crate gives added stimulation and enrichment to the environment. Dogs chew when they are teething (permanent adult teeth start to erupt at four months), stressed, bored, or just for the fun of it. Provide toys that if chewed will not harm your dog, and provide toys with different textures to satisfy their need to chew. This also allows you to offer blankets for warmth and cushion and provides your dog a comfortable place with his or her scent on it. Materials should be easy to remove and easy to launder. Providing chew toys in the crate will most often deter "chewers" from shredding their bedding. Do not ever associate the crate with punishment.

You have established the den space, now we need the elimination space. When choosing the site of elimination, there are a few factors to bear in mind. First, make the spot you choose close and convenient for you and the dog. When you first get up in the morning, you do not want to hike to the bathroom, and sometimes, you cannot make it. When you gotta go, you gotta go! This holds true for dogs, too, and they may have to eliminate almost immediately, especially if they get excited or have been crated for a long period. You may have to carry your puppy outside early on until they can make it past the door.

Try to choose a relatively close outdoor space and take the dog to this spot consistently. You can start your puppy out on a leash to lead it to this spot, then, calmly say a trigger phrase that you choose. For example, you may something like, "Go potty," "Do your business," or any short phase that you want to say to the dog every time you want it to eliminate waste. As the puppy is sniffing and acting like he or she may be getting ready to go, calmly reiterate, "Good dog, go potty." Immediately upon the dog starting to eliminate, reward in a soft, calm voice (as to not excite and distract your dog) say "Good boy (or girl), good potty." Right after the puppy has finished, you can use more enthusiasm here and really make a big deal of it — "Gooood boy! Good potty, good boy!" Very soon, your puppy will begin to associate these key trigger words with eliminating and the positive reinforcement of doing it in the right place.

There are products available in spray or liquid form that contain the odor of urine, such as Puppy Housebreaking Aid, that you can place on the site where you want the puppy to go. These strong odors will be a strong instinctual indicator that this is the site to eliminate in. You may start to add in specific terms for what your puppy does. For example as he is defecating, "Good poop, good boy." Use the same technique of reward as described above. This can be a real asset when you are traveling with your pet in unfamiliar places, and he will be encouraged to eliminate in these new areas. You may feel a little silly at times making such a big deal about the "business," but it is an important part of positive reinforcement and consistency that will help your puppy learn quickly. We all like being rewarded when we do something good, and your housetraining will move a lot quicker as your puppy thrives on your positive attention.

Many people who have yards or a lawn are very proud, and protective, of their beauty and maintenance. Dogs love to eat, roll on, play, dig, and eliminate on them. So, always be a good neighbor and do not let your dog eliminate on someone else's lawn, and if it does happen, apologize and pick up the waste immediately. Urine contains nitrogen that can scald or "burn" lawns and leave unsightly brown or dead spots of grass. Female dogs can especially cause these burned spots because they squat and tend to put all their concentrated urine in one spot. Grasses such as fescue and perennial ryegrass are more tolerant of urine scald, while Bermuda grass and bluegrass are more sensitive. Clovers, such as white clover or strawberry clover, are easy to maintain and are a good substitute for grass, require less water, require less fertilization, and can better tolerate the harsh effects of urine.

CHAPTER **5**

What to Feed My Puppy

But before you start worrying about where your dog is going to eliminate waste, you have to get there first. That means feeding your dog properly.

Dogs are opportunistic omnivores if left to fend for food themselves. This means that they will eat whatever they can, whenever they can. Our domestic dogs are descendents of the gray wolf. Dr. David Mech, one of the world's most respected experts on the wolf, noted that an 80-pound wolf can eat up to 22 pounds of meat in one session or may fast up to six months. A wolf's diet is primarily meat, almost all protein with some fat.

Diet is a major factor in your puppy's health and proper growth. Puppy foods are specially formulated with the proper balance of calcium and phosphorous to ensure proper bone development. This is why you should always feed puppy food and not adult food to puppies. Puppies can begin eating some solid foods as early as 4 weeks. Feeding puppy food should continue through

the growth of your puppy, usually finishing by about age 9 to 12 months, depending on breed. Breed considerations are important in determining the amount of food your puppy eats or calories it needs. The energy needs per pound of body weight of a Pomeranian are twice that of the needs of a Great Dane.

There are puppy, maintenance, and special diets to meet the needs of many dogs. Puppy and maintenance diets may be breed specific to address the special anatomy and nutrition of individual breeds, such as large or toy breeds. Maintenance diets can be used in adult dogs, or calorie-restricted weight loss diets can be used for overweight dogs. There are several special diets to address dogs with medical conditions such as diabetes or kidney disease. The correct amount to feed your dog depends on the breed, size, activity level, age, temperament, and climate. You can use the recommendations on the food bag as a starting place, then adjust the amounts if your puppy seems overly hungry or starts getting too chubby.

You should feed your dog distinct "meals" and not leave the food down all day. Meal requirements change as the dog grows up:

- Puppies from weaning to 3 months do well on four meals a day.

- At 3 to 6 months of age, you can feed three meals per day.

- At 6 to 12 months, feed your dog two times a day.

- As an adult, you can feed your dog one to two times per day.

Feeding distinct meals allows you to observe and know what and how much your dog is eating, and when he or she is not. You may immediately know that something is not right if your dog refuses to eat its meal. Feeding meals prevents a finicky or picky eater. Leave the food down for 10 to 15 minutes, then pick up any remaining food, and do not offer again until next mealtime. This will help reinforce a schedule and motivation for your dog to eat at your chosen designated meal times. It is not recommended to change your dog's food frequently. This will encourage digestive upset and a finickier appetite. Feed your dog at the same time, in the same place, from the same clean bowl, in a place with minimum distractions each day.

What you feed your puppy also greatly affects how much and how often he or she will eliminate waste. Some foods high in fat or grains may cause diarrhea, as will excess amounts of canned foods. Choosing high-quality protein sources with few grains or byproducts or with added probiotics will aid in the digestibility of the food and the energy your puppy can get through the diet. There are diets specific for large breed dogs, and these diets restrict some of the fat to prevent these puppies from growing so quickly that they experience bone and growth-plate problems. Lower quality diets will move too quickly through your puppy, causing diarrhea, frequent stools, excess odor, gas, or bloating.

Many high-quality dog foods exist on the market today, and almost all have special formulations for puppies or breed types. You can feed your puppy canned foods but realize that too much may be too rich for your puppy's digestive tract. It can be mixed with dry food to increase the fiber content and digestibility. For the long term, dry food helps keep a dog's teeth clean and is better for overall dental health. Many small breed dogs especially have significant dental disease, often because they have been fed canned food all their lives. Remember, when you choose a food that agrees with your puppy, you want to try to stick with it. Sudden diet changes or new protein sources can set off a cascade of digestive upset and diarrhea. If you do decide to change diets, mix the new food gradually with the new food over seven to ten days until you are feeding only the new food. This will give your puppy's digestive tract some time to adjust and avoid uncomfortable upsets. Try to avoid foods with grain (corn and wheat) as the first and main ingredient. These foods may cause excessive gas and bloating and may even trigger some food allergies.

Puppies do not have complete development of organ and muscle function at an early age, and this dictates how often they must eat and eliminate to maintain proper blood sugar and kidney function.

Keeping clean, fresh water available at all times is very important to maintain hydration. Water should be offered all day, but during the early phases of housetraining (up until 10 weeks or so), you may restrict the water to distinct times. When you offer water to the puppy during the day, let it drink as much as it wants, but until its body matures, you must take the puppy outside within 15 to 20 minutes to allow him or her to urinate. Do not practice water deprivation to prevent urine accidents. Offering your puppy water under your observation allows you to correctly time waste elimination to prevent accidents. You may take up the water one hour before bedtime and allow your puppy to urinate one more time before you both go to bed to prevent overnight accidents. You are asking for trouble (urinary infections, excessive drinking and vomiting, or dehydration) if you withhold water from your dog. Mixing water in the food will help maintain good hydration, and many puppies do better if their dry kibble has been premoistened to soften it.

CHAPTER 6

When You Should Start Housetraining

You have made it to this chapter, so you may be asking yourself "when do I start?" The answer is "now!" Puppies should be introduced to their new family pack as early as 8 weeks old. This is a time when strong social bonds are made. A dog matures very quickly compared with a human child. Four months of canine time is equivalent to four years of a child's life. Consider this when you are house-training your puppy because human toddlers do not begin to be potty-trained until 2 years old, and the average child is not fully potty-trained until age 4. The average puppy is housetrained by 4 months of age, but remember each is an individual and learns at different rates. You have the tools here to start this process the day you bring your new puppy home. You have prepared the home, the crate, and the outdoor space for elimination, and you are ready to begin.

Puppies go through some critical phases of growth and learning in the first 12 weeks of life. From birth until at least 8 weeks of age, a puppy needs to be with its mother and siblings to learn social skills, cleanliness, and nurturing behavior. By 3 to 4 weeks of age, the puppy becomes aware of its surroundings as it can see and hear and its sense of smell is becoming more acute. Pups at this age also begin to play with siblings by barking, tail wagging, and biting each other. By age 4 to 5 weeks, the puppy is walking and running quickly but has very little stamina. The puppy chases and plays prey-killing games with his siblings and mother, and begins pawing, baring teeth, and growling. By age 5 to 7 weeks, the mother begins to wean the puppies. The puppies are playing dominance games at this age and are very curious about their environment. By age 7 weeks, all of a puppy's senses are developed, and he or she becomes even braver in the investigation of the environment. At 8 weeks old, puppies will experience a more cautious approach to new items, may become fearful, and startle easily. This is an important lesson in survival as they quickly learn what is good and what could be dangerous and hurt them. Between age 8 and 16 weeks, a puppy needs to be introduced to the outside world, including other people, other dogs, other pets, and new experiences. The puppy should be brought into the "human pack" to allow bonding with new pack members. This often is referred to as the "critical period" that prevents fearful and nonsocial behavior.

The age of your puppy greatly affects how long it can go between elimination times. Young puppies do not have fully developed intestinal muscles and must relieve themselves frequently. Very young puppies typically nurse their mother for one to four minutes every three hours. Puppies can begin eating some solid foods at age 4 weeks and are weaned by 7 to 9 weeks old. Make sure your puppy is eating solid foods and what the previous owner or shelter was feeding. You will want to stick with that food, and if you decide to change, then mix the old and new diets together over a seven- to ten-day period. By 8 to 10 weeks old, your puppy will be eating every four to six hours, urinating within ten to 15 minutes after drinking or eating, and defecating within 30 minutes. Be prepared early on to be taking your puppy out two to three times during the night. By about 10 to 12 weeks of age, the puppy may need out only once at night and able to hold it through the night by age 3 to 4 months. It is important to take the age of your puppy into consideration when housetraining, as the age will dictate how often your puppy must eliminate.

Realize that every movement and action that your dog observes from you is part of its life training. Vilmos Csanyi in 2005 "Canine Intel" wrote:

"A family dog constantly observes human behavior and always tries to predict interesting actions in which he could participate. Dogs can learn any tiny signal for the important actions and are always ready to contribute.

Questioning is very important in human group behavior. To pose a question is to show interest in the thoughts of someone else. Young dogs also question us: Where do we go? Which way? Who is coming? Who goes down with me? Is it permitted? And so on. If people are careful and answer the questions, it can soon become a regular method of communication with the dog. If questions do not get attention, dogs give up, just like human children."

Dogs are instinctively pack animals and will look to their leader, or alpha, for guidance and leadership. Use this leadership in your body language and correction techniques, and your dog will soon respect its "fair" leader.

Basic Commands

Before we start on the techniques of housetraining, we first must address some basic obedience commands to help better control and guide your puppy. Obedience training can alleviate behavioral problems and help your puppy trust and respect you. The basic commands of sit, come, stay, leave it, and kennel up are very basic but essential commands that will help you have effective communication with your puppy.

Correcting behavior

Correcting an unwanted behavior requires real vigilance on your part. A correction decreases the likelihood of a behavior happening again. The criteria you must follow when correcting your puppy must be:

1) The correction must be delivered within seconds of the onset of the unwanted behavior.

2) The correction must be delivered every time the unwanted behavior occurs.

3) The correction should interrupt the unwanted behavior but should not induce aggressive or fearful behavior in the dog.

This technique of correction can be accomplished through your voice or remotely, like a squirt from a water gun or a loud noise, such as a shaker can, a hairdryer, air horn, or a motion-activated alarm. Be careful using these methods with dogs that scare easily or are overly sensitive because these loud noises may cause excess fear in the dog.

In addition to a tremendous sense of smell, a dog's hearing is much greater than ours. A dog can hear higher frequencies than humans and can even hear the vibrations of an insect behind a wall. They can hear the pulse of the crystal resonator in a digital alarm clock. This enhanced sense of hearing creates an environment that is much louder and has more sounds than what humans hear. So, it is not necessary to shout out commands to your dog; they can hear you even at a whisper. The ears of a dog show the level of attention to the situation at hand. Erect ears standing at attention show that the dog is engaged and listening to a particular sound. Ears that are slightly pulled back indicate a friendly pose, and ears that are pulled tightly back against the head indicate the dog is timid, shy, or afraid.

Starting to Train Your Puppy

Starting with a leash and knowing how to walk with it allows you to control and guide your puppy to where you want it to go. If your puppy is not familiar with a leash, hook it on its collar and let it walk around on its own for awhile, letting him or her go and making sure it does not become entangled or caught on anything. Next, hold the leash and walk around with it following your puppy. After the puppy becomes familiar with the leash, hold it, say come, and gently urge the puppy toward you. Do not jerk or drag the leash. As your puppy begins to come to you, give lots of praise or even a treat. Now you may begin walking and holding the leash, encouraging your dog to follow and walk with you.

The "sit" command is easy to teach and helps to "reset" the puppy's mindset to a time to pay attention as to what comes next. It lets you keep the puppy from jumping on others and running amok. It is a command that can be used before instigating another action, such as setting down the food, hooking on the leash, or meeting a stranger. A puppy that sits on command is a polite puppy.

Start with a food treat, and get your puppy's attention by having him or her look at you and smell the treat. Raise the treat over and back of your puppy's head, and say the word "sit" in a calm voice. As his nose begins to follow, his head will go back and his hind end down into a seated position. This is using gravity and mechanics to your benefit. As soon as the puppy is seated, give him or her the treat, and reward with praise and the cue word combined, "Good boy, good sit, good sit!"

The "come" command can be very challenging for pet owners. You may know other dogs that do not come on command and

tend to ignore their owners pleading. As you can imagine, it is one of the most important commands a dog should know for their protection to prevent wandering or getting lost or hurt. Dogs need a positive reinforcement for a task to be completed. You can use a food treat as a motivating factor at first and exuberance in your voice to reinforce it.

Hold a treat and call your dog's name and the cue, "Come Archie, come!" As soon as your dog starts toward you, begin rewarding with verbal "good boy, come." Give the puppy the treat and lots of praise when he or she comes to you. Another good tactic is to play the hide and seek game and call the dog again, but while you are out of sight from the dog. This will become a seeking game that the puppy will enjoy, and he gets lots of praise and a treat when he finds you. For better control, some people may begin this exercise on a long leash line to prevent the puppy from wandering or getting distracted.

Sit Command

To teach the sit command, get your dog's focus with a treat and say the word "sit." As you say the word, you can slightly raise the treat above and behind the dog's head. As he watches and follows the treat upward with his head, the position of his body will naturally go into a sit. You can help your puppy by placing him in the sit position the first couple of times to help him understand. Give lots of praise immediately when he does it correctly, and reward with food treat.

CHAPTER 7

Techniques Used to Housetrain a Puppy

arlier in chapter 3, we touched on the importance of a crate, or den space, for the safety of your puppy and your home. The crate is to become the safety zone for your puppy, which will likely seek it out even when you do not force the issue. The crate should be in a desirable spot that provides adequate ventilation and visualization of the family "pack." Do not isolate the puppy in a separate room where there is no activity. The crate needs to be comfortable for sleeping, and big enough to stand up, turn around, lie down, and stretch out. You may feed and water your puppy in the crate and provide toys for play. Feeding your dog in the crate will help reinforce it as your dog's private, safe, and desirable place. In the beginning, you may not want to feed and water your puppy in the crate because this will stimulate the digestive process and defeat your housetraining efforts. Once a puppy is housetrained, you may then be able to provide access to food and water. A dog does not want to eliminate where it eats or sleeps, so the crate is a great motivating factor to learn how to "hold it." Upon immediate release from the crate, the dog should be taken outdoors, given the verbal cue, and allowed to eliminate.

Comfort in the Crate

If your puppy is not already used to the crate, you can simplify this process through some basic positive reinforcement. Provide a safe toy in the crate that your puppy can play with and chew on. Do not place paper in the crate because this may encourage elimination in the crate, especially if a breeder who used paper pads raised the puppy. Use a trigger word, such as "time for kennel," and place the puppy in the crate with a food treat. Stay in the same room as the puppy, then, after five minutes, release the puppy from the crate, and give praise. Do not release the puppy when he or she is barking or "acting out" because this will only encourage the wrong behavior. Repeat this task several times per day. The next day, increase the time to ten minutes, and build daily in five-minute increments until the puppy can be quiet and comfortable alone for 30 minutes. This task will help the puppy develop confidence and independence in the crate and in knowing that you will return. Now, the puppy should be able to sleep overnight in the crate without fear or bad behavior.

Waste Elimination Alternatives

There are other alternatives to eliminating outdoors. You may want an indoor alternative if you live in the city or an apartment, are elderly or handicapped, have a small dog, travel, own a young puppy that does not have good muscle control of its bladder or bowels, or have a geriatric dog that cannot hold its urine or has trouble getting outdoors. The other options you may then consider are paper or potty pad or litter pan training. Housetraining and paper training are two different practices, and each has its own rules and requirements. Housetraining is teaching the dog that it is never appropriate to eliminate indoors, while paper training encourages indoor elimination. Paper training is not used to teach outdoor elimination. Paper training is an aid for eliminating indoors that you can clean up easily and is best suited for toy and small breed dogs or for city dwellers that may not have regular access to an outdoor area. Potty pads are moisture-proof pads that have a plastic sheet backing that protects surfaces from soiling. Like the outdoor designated area, the pad can become a more defined space for elimination. Take the puppy to the pad, and use your trigger phrase. You may encourage elimination on the pad by placing urine or fecal odor on the pad. This will suggest that this is a spot to eliminate on. Newspapers should be stacked at least ten sheets thick placed over a plastic bag that is cut open and laid out to prevent urine from soaking through. Litter pans can be lined with paper and is another elimination option for toy breed dogs. You also may use the pad in the crate when your puppy is very young or you have to leave him or her for longer periods that may necessitate waste elimination; however, try to avoid this if you can because you do not want to encourage this behavior in the crate. Use the same technique when training on paper as you would outdoors — lead your puppy to the site, use your trigger phrase to initiate elimination, and praise. Always remember to keep the elimination site away from the food, water, and sleeping area

If your puppy was raised in a "puppy mill," he or she likely was not allowed outside of the kennel or crate very often, if at all. As a result, the puppy was forced to eliminate and soil where he or she slept. Puppies that were removed too early from their mother also do not learn to be clean and may learn to soil where they sleep. These circumstances may make your puppy more difficult to train using the crate. In these cases, you may seek other options, such as an exercise pen, a safe room with baby gates, litter pans, or even a box of sod to learn to eliminate in these new areas rather than in the sleeping space.

A Designated Elimination Spot

If you take your puppy outside to its designated elimination spot and it does not go, put the puppy back into the crate for 15 minutes, then take outside again to the spot. Your puppy needs to learn that you take him or her to this spot for a good reason, and meandering around or playing is not allowed. Repeat these steps by taking your puppy on the leash to the elimination spot, and if he or she does not "do business," take the puppy back inside and into the crate. Do this in 15-minute intervals, and soon your dog will realize what is expected on these "potty breaks." As a good rule of thumb, always take your puppy outside to eliminate first thing in the morning, after each meal and drink of water, after exercise and play periods, after a nap, before bedtime, and anytime he or she starts sniffing for a place to go.

Eventually, you will not want to always have to leash your puppy to escort to the elimination site. You can start by giving your puppy a little more freedom by walking, off leash, to the site, and use your verbal cue. Gradually, over a week, walk with your dog (off leash), bring your leash just in case, and accompany your puppy to the spot. The next week, accompany your puppy three-fourths of the way to the area, and make sure your dog continues the rest of the way alone. The next week, walk only halfway toward the site, and the following week only one-fourth of the way. Of course, make sure your body language still conveys what you want, and continue your lavish praise when eliminating in the proper spot. Eventually, you will be able to let your dog outside and watch him or her eliminate waste from the door. This is only an option for those who have fenced yards or large pieces of property. Do not attempt this technique if you live in a busy city or apartment complex — keep your dog on a leash for protection from harm. Remember, always pick up the poop, and do not let more than two piles accumulate in the designated area. An elimination site soiled with feces may discourage your dog from going in that spot. If your dog goes to another area of the yard (that you do not want), do not correct this because it may cause fear of eliminating outdoors. Instead, get the puppy to the proper site by calling his or her name and trotting yourself to the site, "Sam, come Sam, come do your business!" Remember to praise. Next time, you may want to usher him or her to the site again with encouragement before he or she goes to another part of the yard.

Reward-Based Training

Making the right thing easy (and rewarded) and the wrong thing difficult (using correction) is the basis for reward-based training. We have already touched on the importance of vocal praise and encouragement, in an upbeat tone. Reward training gives the dog association between doing something and a positive reward associated with the action. Clicker training is also used to reward the right action. Prior training must be used for the dog to associate its positive actions with the clicking noise. Food reward training is also an immediate positive gratification for doing the right thing. One of the drawbacks to food or clicker training is that the item must always be with you when you reward the action, and that may not always be possible. Several training guides can give you more information on how to use these other reward techniques. When you correct your dog, all you will need to say is "no." Do not hit your dog with a rolled up newspaper or your hand, and do not rub a dog's nose in his excrement or abuse him physically. Only correct the action if you catch the dog in the act, and never punish for something after the fact. Because dogs live in the moment, they do not associate the punishment with something they did before or feel remorse for something that happened in the past (even if it was just a couple of minutes ago).

Your dog will start to give you cues naturally that he or she needs to go outside if you observe closely. Some puppies, after a couple of weeks, may start to go to the door and stand, sit, bark, or scratch at the door when they need to go. You also can teach your dog to signal with a bark or whine. Start by having your dog practice the come, sit, and stay commands to get his brain in the "learning" mode. Then, to teach the "speak" command, say "speak" and hold a treat up and gently tease the puppy until he or she makes even the smallest sound, then reward immediately. You can work this up to a full-fledged bark.

Then, when your dog knows the "speak" command, you can transfer this to association with the door. When you get ready to take your dog outside the next time, clip on the leash but do not open the door yet. Create motivation and excitement about going outdoors and say, "Speak." At the first sign of even a whine or vocalization in anticipation, open the door and immediately praise, "Good boy, good speak!" The dog will soon make the connection that the bark results in the door opening. Once your dog has learned the speak command at the door, do not use treats anymore. Your petting and praise will be reward enough, and we do not want to teach him that going to the door gets him treats. This will result in a dog that runs and barks at the door every time he wants a treat. You also can use a bell for your dog to signal that he needs to go out. Hang a large bird bell or sleigh bell on a piece of string or ribbon and hang it from the handle of the door. When your dog wants to go out, first have him or her sit at the door, and then lift a paw to touch the bell and say, "ring." As soon as the bell makes a sound, open the door and praise, "Good boy, good ring!" Eventually your dog will lift a paw and touch the bell or ring it with his or her nose to signal the need to go outside.

It cannot be overstressed or said enough how invaluable a tool that praise is. It is not necessarily the words you are using, it is the tone of your voice, and the body language you are exhibiting. If your friend has her arms crossed and a stern look on her face when you asked her if "something was wrong," and she said, "no," would you believe her? Her words may have indicated that nothing is wrong, but her body language clearly spoke volumes about her true feelings. Your dog is a very astute reader of body language and posture and listening. Make sure that your body posture is relaxed, that you are not staring the dog down, and that you speak in a clear, soothing, encouraging tone. It is not suggested to use the dog's name when reprimanding or correcting the action of your dog as this may associate his name with a negative outcome. Any method of correction that occurs after the fact will only make it more difficult to train your dog, and may result in a dog that is fearful or afraid to eliminate in front of you. Be vigilant about supervising your dog both indoors and outdoors, allowing you to praise or correct the behavior in an immediate manner.

The Potty Picture

Now that you have a designated area picked out and have established reward-based training, it is time to talk about the big subject. Some people just do not want to talk about this subject — the subject of elimination. Some people are grossed out or just plain uncomfortable talking about bodily functions. But, this is one of the most common questions veterinarians ask about pets. "Are there any changes in drinking or urination? How do the feces look? Is there any diarrhea or vomiting?" These are such important components of overall health that veterinarians often look to these symptoms as indicators of a problem or disease. So, with that said, do not be embarrassed to inspect it, notice it, know how much, how often, and what it looks like. Your puppy and your veterinarian will be grateful that you know the answers to these awkward questions.

Up until about 5 weeks of age, their mother must stimulate them to help them eliminate. After this, they will begin to wander away from the den or nest to find a place to eliminate. They will need to urinate after waking and have a bowel movement within 30 minutes of eating.

When you know what your puppy's urination and fecal patterns look like, you are inspecting for general health and well-being. It can tell you whether everything appears OK, if there is reason for concern, what your dog is eating, and how it is digesting. Normal urination is light yellow in color and is a steady stream that lasts a few seconds, then stops. Females and young male dogs usually squat to urinate, and older males may lift their leg when urinating. Normal feces are formed well, light brown in color, often segmented, and should be expelled with little effort. Changes in these patterns can be an important indicator of a problem, and this will significantly affect housetraining efforts.

Keep an eye out for abnormal patterns and what they could mean. Stranguria, straining to urinate, is common with urinary tract infections, partial blockages, blood in urine, bladder tumors, or discomfort when urinating. The dog may initially look like it is urinating normally but then stays in the squat position with only small drips of urine. The dog may walk on and quickly squat again and attempt to urinate. These dogs feel the sensation to urinate even though their bladders may be empty. They may exhibit urine dripping or dribbling, or excessive licking.

Tenesmus, or straining to defecate, is common when a dog is having diarrhea, constipation, or trying to pass a foreign object. A veterinary associate once saw a lab pass a whole Barbie doll! You just never know what is coming out unless you look. The dog may have to defecate more often, feel like it is never quite finished, or may walk as it is attempting to defecate. The volume of feces passed may be voluminous or scant, have a very foul odor, or even contain blood.

Steatorrhea, or oily feces, leaves a glistening oily residue or rancid odor, which can indicate maldigestion of fats, often due to a pancreatic enzyme deficiency. Excess gas, or borbyrgmus, can indicate digestive upset and bloating or an over active intestinal tract. Observe the feces for signs of foreign bodies such as plastic, aluminum foil, bone fragments, fiber, or other things that you may have not known that your puppy ate. If you observe any of these abnormal behaviors or eliminations, let your veterinarian know so that the problem can be fixed. Save a fresh sample of the stool or the urine if you can, or put in fridge overnight, so the vet can test the feces or urine for any problems.

The Behavior of Elimination

Dogs communicate through olfactory, visual, and vocal cues to other dogs. Dogs use their body language to communicate visually to other dogs. At 8 to 10 weeks old, a puppy must eliminate every hour. By age 4 months, the puppy needs to go seven to eight times per day, and an adult dog goes three to five times per day. Puppies reach sexual maturity by 4 to 6 months, and all puppies should be housetrained by age 6 months. Small breed dogs mature faster than large breed dogs and certain breeds can be harder to train. Male puppies tend to take longer than females to housetrain due to their tendency toward marking behavior. You can begin to read and anticipate a dog's body language and posture before a dog eliminates.

The sense of smell

The sense of smell in a dog is one of the most remarkable physical qualities of the canine species. A dog's nose is the equivalent to our fingerprint with a pattern of ridges and dimples that give a unique print to each dog. As a dog ages, often it will lose its sense of hearing or sight, but its sense of smell usually remains for a lifetime. Humans see the world first through vision to make sense of our world of sounds. Dogs, on the other hand, use smell as their first observation of the world to make sense of what they hear and see. The result is an animal that "sees" via its nose rather than its eyes. Dogs have a specialized vomeronasal organ (VNO) in the roof of their mouth that allows them to detect and intensify the smell of pheromones that are vital to maternal care and sexual behavior. Dogs will flick their tongue in and out, as if drinking, to intensify to smell and gather it to the VNO. A dog's sense of smell is 1,000 to 100,000 times stronger than a human's. Human noses have 6 million sensory receptors sites in their nasal passages, but dogs have up to 300 million. This allows a dog to detect a teaspoon of sugar dissolved in a million gallons of water, or two Olympic size swimming pools. A dog can detect human scent on a glass slide that has been lightly fingerprinted and left outside for two weeks. Dogs trained in arson detection can sniff out drops of lighter fluid or lamp oil in an environment covered in several inches of water, snow, mud, or fire debris.

Most dogs begin with an intense focused sniffing of the area before they eliminate. They smell for the presence of another dog, urine, or the smell of feces and other odors. A dog postures in a squatting position before urinating. Before having a bowel movement (defecation), a dog may travel to a more distant space and begin circling and then squat with the hind end and spine curved down before defecation. By observing these subtle behaviors, you will be able to correct or redirect the activity to a more desirable area. All puppies should be allowed to eliminate immediately upon exiting the crate, after eating, playing, and upon waking.

Maintain your posture

Your own body posture also communicates a great deal to a dog. Your presence in a relaxed, calm, non-staring, non-intimidating way will help your dog complete its "duty" outside, while still allowing you to observe and praise the action. If a dog senses tension, anger, or intimidating behaviors from its owner, he or she may become fearful to eliminate in front of you. If dogs sense extreme fear, stress, or anxiety, they may urinate, defecate, or express their anal glands. Submissive urination may occur if a dog is trying to communicate its submission to another dog or human and may be associated with a reprimand or upon excitement. This behavior is more common in young female puppies; most puppies will outgrow this behavior by the time they are 1 year old. When accompanying your dog outside, assess your own posture and presence to encourage the correct behavior from your dog. Look for and read the signals that your puppy may show you when he or she needs to eliminate, often exhibited as going to the door, whining, acting restless, intense sniffing on the floor, or circling.

Other behaviors

Other behavior that you will experience with your puppy is the important aspect of play. Different breeds of dogs play differently — herding dogs playing herding games, or terrier breeds playing chase and tug-of-war. Play is exercise for the mind and body and a way to practice instinctual chase and prey-driven behavior. It is fast-paced and coordinated. Certain breeds appear to like playing with other dogs especially of their own breed as they may more able to read these breed-specific ways of play. The play bow is usually the instigator of communicating play to another dog or person. The dog bows with its head down and its rear end up to indicate its willingness to play. Dogs may also take the "stalking" position and lay on their chest with a lowered head, focused gaze, and legs underneath the body before "pouncing" on the play partner.

To differentiate urine-marking behavior from simple urination, the place, surface, and circumstances will offer the answer. Urine marking is often deposited on vertical surfaces (a tree, end of couch, a wall) and involves small quantities of urine on the target. Sexually mature female dogs also can exhibit marking behavior. Limit a dog's exposure to stimuli that may trigger marking behavior, make the target aversive to the dog, and correct immediately when the behavior begins. Neutering male dogs and spaying female dogs often will eliminate this unwanted behavior completely.

Cleanliness Deters Elimination

The home, sleeping, and outdoor environment should be kept as clean as possible to deter dogs from choosing misplaced areas to eliminate. The crate should be kept dry and clean and blankets laundered to prevent repeated elimination in the crate and to prevent bacterial infections on your dog's skin. Outdoor feces should be picked up and disposed of to prevent disease and parasite transmission. When you take your puppy on a walk, you should carry a plastic bag to pick up remove any feces from the walkway, park, road, or neighbor's yard.

Dogs have a tremendous sense of smell, and even a special odor-amplifying organ, the vomeronasal organ, as mentioned earlier. This gives dogs a sense of smell 1,000 times that of humans, and odors that are undetectable to us can be significant stimulus for a dog. Enzyme cleaners are most effective at removing these odors. Enzymes actually breakdown, digest, and destroy odors, not just cover or mask them with another smell. There are many quality nontoxic enzymatic cleaning products on the market today such as Nature's Miracle, Simple Solution® Stain and Odor Remover, Nilodor®, Get Serious® Pet Stain Remover, Nilotex, No Scents, and Housesaver™. Try to clean the urine or fecal odor immediately after an accident occurs to prevent the smell from triggering another episode.

If, and when, your dog has an accident, clean it up immediately with an enzymatic odor neutralizer. When a dog urinates, it initially does not have much odor, but as urine starts to degrade the odor will worsen and become stronger. If you do not properly clean this area and eliminate the odor, it will be a strong trigger for your dog to urinate in this place again. Urine is composed of urea, and this begins to break down into the strong smell of ammonia. Further breakdown produces mercaptans, which creates a very foul odor. Mercaptans are the chemicals that give rotten cabbage and skunk spray its unique potency.

Many pet owners want to keep their puppy smelling fresh at all times and want to bathe the puppy often. Keeping your puppy free from odor and debris is important, however overzealous bathing actually can dry the skin and create a disruption in the protective skin barrier. Try not to bathe your puppy more frequently than once a week, and use gentle, nondrying, non-perfumed products. The presence of dirt, body oils, and food debris may cause bacteria or molds to proliferate in fabrics. Bedding and toys should be laundered immediately if soiled, and every two to three weeks even if not soiled.

CHAPTER **8**

Some Common Misconceptions

Before we discuss how you may establish a schedule for housetraining, you should be familiar with some important facts and misconceptions in knowing what to and what not to expect from your puppy. This information will help alleviate some of the frustrations that may occur during this process. Animal behaviorist Jolanta Benal and author of *The Dog Trainer's Quick and Dirty Tips for Teaching and Caring for Your Pet* describes some of the most common misconceptions that a pet owner may experience and is presented here in summary:

Overestimating Capacity of the Puppy

Many owners make the mistake of overestimating the "carrying" and "holding" capacity of their dog. Puppies often are able to sleep up to eight hours through the night, and owners often expect them to hold it during the day for long periods. Unfortunately, your puppy cannot physically "hold it" this long during the day. During the night, there is very little to no "input" into the puppy — no food or water — and therefore there is no "output." Metabolism and the production of urine and feces also are slowed during sleep.

This is not the case during the day. A puppy will be eating and drinking during the daytime and will be producing waste material as its body metabolizes food into energy. An old rule of thumb used to estimate how long your dog can hold it is the number of hours equal to his age in months plus one. For example, an 8-week-old puppy could, in theory, hold its elimination for two months (8 weeks) plus one, which would be three hours.

Some estimates are more conservative. Information from the San Francisco branch of the Society for the Prevention of Cruelty to Animals (SPCA) provides a housetraining tip sheet that states the maximum time for a 4-month-old puppy is only three hours. It is better for a pet owner always to err on the side of caution to avoid accidents by allowing more elimination breaks. The muscles of young dogs and young humans are not fully developed, and they are not able to hold their bowels or urine for very long periods.

How Many Potty Breaks are Enough?

New dog owners of puppies or older dogs should expect to take their dog out frequently at first. This will help you more quickly get to know your dog's elimination habits. The newborn puppy eliminates every hour when awake. Each week thereafter, you can add another 30 minutes to the time that he or she is able to "hold it." The very young puppy should be allowed to eliminate outside, and then given only a few minutes of freedom in the room before going back into the crate until the next potty break. This is a good way to prevent accidents in the room and teaches the puppy to not eliminate in the resting area. This also helps in the development of the muscles that enable the puppy to control waste elimination.

Some owners may think that once a puppy has eliminated, that he or she is empty and will not need to go again until the next scheduled time. This is not always the case, and it is important to observe your puppy for signs and signals that indicate the need to eliminate again. The three most frequent signs of this behavior include restlessness, circling, and intently sniffing the ground. Puppies will usually eliminate within 15 minutes of eating or drinking and immediately upon waking up. Any activity, such as playing or chewing, will also stimulate elimination, so be sure to take your puppy outside after these activities, too.

Walking the Trainee

Many people who have the time enjoy walking their puppy through the neighborhood or the park. Although walking your dog is a very healthy habit for both you and your dog, it can work against the housetraining process if you are not careful. Before you actually start a walk, the puppy should be allowed to eliminate and praised dearly for doing so. Take the puppy on leash to the elimination site and just stand there. Do not do anything except wait two to three minutes for the puppy to eliminate. As soon as he or she does, praise immediately. If the puppy does not go, take him or her back inside and into the crate, wait 10 to 15 minutes, and go outside to the site again. After waste elimination, it is time to walk as a reward. Prompt elimination is what we want to see happen. Dogs that are taken immediately on a walk are often distracted or overwhelmed with other sights and scents that they may not eliminate. These dogs also may associate that when they are walked and then they do eliminate, they are immediately taken back home and into their crate. These dogs may start to intentionally hold it, just so they can remain outdoors longer. This may lead to a dog that then, when returning to the house, drops the "load" in the house as soon as he or she comes in the door. Use the walk as the reward, not as the elimination time.

Punishing Mistakes

People often react adversely and emotionally to a dog's accident or mistake in the house. Although it is very frustrating, the act of punishing a dog for these mistakes is a major pitfall to the success of your housetraining technique. Never punish any behavior that occurred more than just a couple of seconds ago. Your dog will not make the association between your anger and the act if it is corrected "after the fact." If you scold your puppy in the act of peeing on the new wool rug, he or she does not understand that you are angry for peeing on the nice fabric rug. The puppy is only going to associate big, scary, mad you when eliminating in front of you. This may lead to a puppy that will not eliminate in front of you, even if you want him or her to outside. This may cause fear and anxiety in your puppy as he or she becomes nervous about eliminating any time you are looking. Some trainers suggest an interruption technique such as a "chhhh" sound, a noisemaker (like pennies in a can), a sharp "no," or even a clap. For the more sensitive pup, a more gentle distraction may all that is necessary to interrupt the behavior. The noise should be loud enough to interrupt but not scare or cause fear in the puppy. If you stick to a schedule and observe closely for the behavior before elimination occurs, you will seldom need to use these distraction techniques.

Distraction techniques

You may not be 100 percent effective at getting your puppy to the proper elimination spot every time, but you can interrupt the behavior until you can get him there. If you catch your puppy "in the act," immediately interrupt the behavior with a distraction. Your voice is the simplest, fastest correction you can make; you should say "no, no, no" and promptly take your puppy outside; then say the trigger phase and provide a reward if he or she finishes eliminating outside. Whatever word you choose should be sharp, definite in tone, and relay disapproval. Another distraction tool is noisemakers, such as pennies in a can that you shake when your puppy is behaving inappropriately. Remember, these are not punishments but are distractions to reset your puppy's mind away from the behavior that he or she is engaging in.

The eating of feces, or coprophagia, is a disturbing behavior (mostly to the owners) that a dog may partake in. Some fecal eating is due to the young puppy just "tasting" its environment, experimenting, and learning what is edible and what is not. In nature, a mother dog eats the feces of her young to keep the den space clean and to keep away any scent a predator may smell. However, sometimes this behavior can arise from boredom or even vitamin and mineral deficiencies. If your puppy is on a balanced diet, has many opportunities to play, and you maintain a clean yard, it is unlikely that this behavior will occur. If fecal consumption does become a problem, a flagging technique can be implemented. Place a small landscaping flag next to the fecal matter and when the dog approaches it for a "second look," use a trigger phrase to deter the behavior, such as "leave it" or "no." Soon, approaching the feces and the flag is associated with a negative outcome, and your dog will ignore it. Fecal-oral deterrents can be fed to the dog to make the taste very unpleasant. When using these products, they must be fed to all dogs in the household to cause distaste to all the feces that are available to the offender.

CHAPTER **9**

Establishing the Schedule

By now, you have begun to enlist the tools needed to manage the timing involved in housetraining a new puppy. These first few months can be very demanding, just like having a new baby in the house and making sure all of the needs are met. Your timing is imperative to the success of housetraining. Timing is essential and should dictate when you feed, when you go outside, and how and when you give your praise. Some simple habits will help keep your puppy on schedule and avoid many mistakes.

This early period of housetraining is going to require some alterations to your lifestyle. If you have to work outside the home and leave your puppy in the crate, come home right after work to let him relieve himself. No more hanging out at happy hour. Your sleep schedule is also going to be altered during this time. No more sleeping in. At 4 months of age, your puppy should be able to hold it through the night without an accident, and your precious sleep will start to be yours again.

You should give yourself extra time in the morning and the evening for playtime and lots of interaction and bonding with your puppy. It is important for your puppy to have lots of exercise and attention from you when you are home, so he or she does not become bored, destructive, or anxious while you are gone. A played-out puppy is a relaxed, calm puppy in the crate. Always take your dog outside upon waking in the morning or after naps, before you leave the house, before going into the crate at night, immediately after removing from the crate, upon returning home, before entering another building, and a final time before you and the dog go to bed. Once your dog is completely housetrained, you then can begin to take your puppy on walks or the park for exercise.

Sample timeline for owner who works outside the home, puppy younger than 4 months old:

7:15 a.m.	Wake up and let puppy out of crate for potty.
7:25 a.m.	Feed breakfast to puppy.
7:35 a.m.	Potty break. Put puppy back into crate.
8:00 a.m.	Owner leaves house to go to work.
12:00 p.m.	Owner comes home for lunch or neighbor lets puppy out of crate.
12:10 p.m.	Neighbor feeds puppy lunch.
12:25 p.m.	Neighbor gives puppy a potty break and puts puppy back into crate.
5:15 p.m.	Owner comes home from work and give puppy potty break.

6:15 p.m.	Give puppy another potty break and playtime.
7:15 p.m.	Feed puppy dinner.
7:25 p.m.	Give puppy potty break.
8:45 p.m.	Potty break and playtime.
9:45 p.m.	Final potty break and remove water before bedtime. Put back in crate.

Sample timeline for owner or family member that is home all day, 4 to 6-month-old puppy:

7:30 a.m.	Wake up and take puppy outside to potty.
7:40 a.m.	Bring puppy back inside for supervised play.
8:00 a.m.	Give puppy food and water.
8:30 a.m.	Take outside for potty break.
8:45 a.m.	Supervised playtime with family.
10:00 a.m.	Puppy back into crate if needed while running errand.
12:00 p.m.	Let puppy out of crate to potty, then feed lunch.
12:30 p.m.	Take puppy outside for potty break.
12:40 p.m.	Supervised playtime.
1:30 p.m.	Take outside to potty. Put back into crate if needed.
4:30 p.m.	Let out of crate and outside to potty.
5:00 p.m.	Feed puppy.
5:30 p.m.	Take puppy outside for potty break.
5:40 p.m.	Supervised playtime.

6:15 p.m.	Give water, put puppy back in crate if needed.
8:15 p.m.	Take outside for potty break.
8:25 p.m.	Supervised playtime and family interaction.
9:00 p.m.	Take outside for potty.
9:10 p.m.	Put puppy back into crate for short rest.
10:30 p.m.	Take outside for last potty break, back into crate for bedtime.

Sample timeline for owner with puppy older than 6 months of age:

7:30 a.m.	Let dog out of crate for potty.
7:45 a.m.	Feed dog breakfast and get ready to leave for work.
8:00 a.m.	Put dog in crate. Leave for work.
5:15 p.m.	Arrive home from work and let dog out of crate to potty.
6:45 p.m.	Let dog outside for potty break and play.
7:30 p.m.	Feed dog dinner.
7:45 p.m.	Let outside for potty break.
10:15 p.m.	Let outside for final potty break and back into crate for bedtime.

Sample timeline for older housetrained dog and owner working outside home:

6:45 a.m.	Wake up, take dog outside to potty.

7:15 a.m.	Feed dog and leave unlimited water.
7:45 a.m.	Take outside to potty before leaving for work. Put back in crate or may leave in confined area unattended.
12:15 p.m.	Come home for lunch to let dog out to potty.
5:30 p.m.	Come from work and let dog outside to eliminate.
7:00 p.m.	Feed dog dinner (if eating twice a day).
8:00 p.m.	Let dog outside for potty break.
10:30 p.m.	Let outside again for final potty break before bedtime. Place dog back in crate if appropriate for night.

Consistency is critical to success, so you should stick to the schedule you develop during this period. A dog must practice a behavior at least 40 times for it to be committed to long-term memory. So, the old adage that "practice makes perfect" stands true. Finding your own key words helps you also establish consistency and repetition in your commands. Consider these words carefully because they always should be on the tip of your tongue, and choose something that you would not be embarrassed to say in a public place where others may hear you. "Do your business," "go potty," and "do your duty" are short, easy, non-offensive, and you will be saying them often. Be creative, but always remember to be consistent.

Exercise is often an underrated component of a dog's training. Exercise stimulates the brain, releases energy, is a natural healthy part of canine behavior and socialization, and stimulates the digestive tract. And, yes, dogs need sunshine to get a sufficient amount of Vitamin D. Veterinarians may prescribe "sunshine therapy" to a dog that was deficient, and this could make a tremendous difference in his or her health. So, do not disregard exercise and play. Schedule it into your puppy's training, and you will have a much calmer, focused, responsive, and well-adjusted puppy. Dogs need exercise to be mentally, emotionally, and physically fit.

Supervised free time is a time for the puppy to interact and observe his or her family pack and to explore new sights, sounds, smells, and activities. Your puppy should always be under your vision to prevent destructive behavior and accidents. Provide this free time only after your puppy has eaten and been outside to urinate and defecate. This will help ensure that the "pipes are empty" as he or she explores new freedoms.

The value of praise for doing the right thing, right when it happens cannot be emphasized enough. Praise can take many forms and does not need to only be with your voice. Different types of reward incentives for you dog may be:

- Petting, massaging, or some other physical attention

- Approval with the tone of your voice, special phrases, smiles and laughter

- A special treat

- A favorite toy or game

- The joy of the activity

- Your silent but obvious approval with body language

The initial four to five months of your puppy's schedule to eliminate may seem daunting at first, so do not be afraid to elicit some help from your family members, friends, and coworkers. Having someone give you a break sometimes is a good way to stay motivated in your training. Make sure that whomever you have help knows your chosen trigger phrases, feeding, and elimination schedules. There are three basic premises that you are trying to teach: It is good to eliminate outside, it is bad to eliminate inside, and these rules apply to all indoor places (not just his or her home). The timeline above is an example of a schedule that gives you ideas on how to divide your time. Your work or family situation may dictate some different timing, but the essence of the schedule is to have one.

CHAPTER 10

When Accidents Happen

Despite all your best efforts, accidents will happen. These are teaching opportunities for you and not the puppy. Here are some things to think about and troubleshoot what went wrong.

Evaluate your timing. Were you watching your puppy closely or was it out of your immediate sight? How about your body posture and language? Did you look intimidating, act angry, speak loudly, shout, or cause excessive excitement to your puppy? If you did not catch the dog in the act, do not punish him. He cannot relate his natural behavior to a time in the past that made you mad. You must catch the puppy in the "act" to correct it.

If your puppy has eliminated in its crate, reevaluate the crate space. Is it too big, so the puppy can relieve itself in one end and sleep in the other? Is it clean and odor-free so it does not stimulate the behavior? Did you put papers in the crate or feed and water your puppy in the crate and not take him or her outside in a timely manner? How much time was your puppy in the crate, and was it allowed to eliminate waste outside? How old is your puppy, and can he or she really "hold it" that long? If your puppy had an accident in another part of the home, he or she may not necessarily recognize this space as inside home space, especially if the puppy is not familiar with the room. Introduce your

puppy slowly and repetitively to more spaces in the house and interact with the puppy so he or she soon recognizes it as an "inside" space in which not to eliminate.

Odors are a significant stimulus for dogs and can persist in the environment for a long time. Did you properly clean, and not just mask, prior odors in the carpet or bedding? Was the site of elimination an area that was previously marked by either your dog or another? Did you properly choose a designated area to eliminate in, or does the puppy have free roam of its environment? If you have used all the proper odor removal steps and your dog still keeps eliminating on this spot, you may try feeding your dog at this site to discourage this behavior. Because a dog does not like to eliminate where he eats, this technique uses natural behavior to your benefit to modify the problem. Continue feeding your dog at least a week at this spot before reverting to his original feeding spot. If the problem reoccurs, repeat feeding at this spot. Adult dogs that have a long history of this inappropriate elimination may take up to six weeks to retrain.

Distractions abound for puppies as they are exploring a new environment and thinking, "the world is my oyster." Were there interruptions to the schedule or new people or pets in the household? Was there a lot of excitement and play occurring? Was the puppy preoccupied the last time he or she was outside and did not eliminate? It takes focus for a puppy to know when and where it needs to go to eliminate, and puppies are easily distracted by these other factors. Remember to lead your puppy to the site, give your cue, and do not dance around the subject — he should eliminate within five minutes of being taken to the spot.

Try not to confuse your puppy by initiating play or any other activity until he or she has relieved himself.

If your dog has marked on your bed, clothing, armchair, on the baby's toys, on another dog's bed, or even you, your dog is most likely trying to establish dominance over you and your (and in the puppy's mind, his or her) things. This is unacceptable behavior, and neutering likely will stop this from continuing. Further training and leadership exercises will establish your role as pack leader and earn respect from your dog.

When you take your puppy to a new or unfamiliar place, he or she may not recognize it as you do as an "off-limit" zone for elimination. The puppy may recognize that it is not correct to eliminate in his or her home space, but this is not the home space. To avoid these mistakes in your neighbor's home or a place of business, make sure to give your puppy an opportunity to eliminate outdoors before entering a new place. You must teach him that eliminating in any indoor place, not just the home, is wrong.

If you have gone through your checklist and cannot find any human error to the accident occurring, then your dog may have a medical or behavioral condition. The behavioral conditions that can cause house soiling are anxiety-related elimination, excitement urination, submissive urination, urine marking, or cognitive dysfunction syndrome.

Dogs with anxiety-related elimination show this behavior when they experience extreme fear or surprise or are separated from their owners (separation anxiety). Other signs of stress such as excessive panting, pacing, vocalization, destruction, or escape behavior often accompany separation anxiety. Puppies may express their anal glands, urinate, or defecate.

Submissive urination usually occurs in young dogs. It occurs as a signal of submission to other dogs or humans. The puppy will often have its ears back, avoid eye contact, cower, or roll over. Puppies may dribble or squirt small amounts of urine. Most puppies outgrow this behavior by about 7 months of age, but it can occur at any age. To minimize this behavior, owners and other people should greet the puppy in a less-threatening manner by kneeling down, averting their eyes, and petting under the chest and not over the head. When arriving home, do not greet or make eye contact with your dog immediately, wait at least five minutes and let your dog settle down. Crouch down to your dogs level to approach and pet him, do not bend over. Guests should not greet the dog, and should sit down. They should not approach the dog. As the dog approaches them, they should speak softly and not make eye contact. Avoid any reprimands or harsh tone in your voice. As your puppy grows, most will develop more confidence and outgrow these conditions. You should never punish your puppy for submissive urination because this may only worsen the problem. You can engage the puppy in another activity, such as tossing a ball or giving it a sit command, to divert this behavior.

Urine marking can occur even when adequate opportunity has been given to the dog for urination. The dog often lifts his or her leg, and urine is deposited in small quantities, usually on a vertical surface. Some female dogs also mark in the squatting position. Marking behavior may start at 3 months of age. Marking territory outside is a dog's way of indicating to other members his or her territory and dominance within the pack and acts like a "calling card" to others. This behavior is common in unaltered male dogs and is often triggered by a female dog in estrus, other dog or pet, or a new item or person in the household. This behavior often begins with the onset of sexual maturity at 6 to 24 months. This is not a housetraining problem, but a behavioral problem. Dogs that are urine marking are trying to establish their dominance over a territory. These dogs may exhibit this behavior due to the presence of another male urine odor, the presence of females in estrus, jealousy over a new pet or baby, a visitor in the house, or when they feel anxious or nervous about a new situation and want to express their dominance. Neutering a male dog, making the targets averse, and limiting a dog's exposure to these stimuli will help curtail this behavior. Allowing your dog more exercise and outside time will give these dogs many opportunities to mark outdoors rather than indoors. Neutering your pet before the onset of sexual maturity at age 6 months will help eliminate this behavior before it becomes a habit.

Cognitive dysfunction syndrome as a cause of house soiling occurs in elderly dogs usually older than 7 years of age. This is a form of canine senility, and dogs may "forget" to ask to outside and eliminate in the house, even though they were previously housetrained. This behavior is often accompanied by other signs such as getting lost in the house, changes in social behavior, disorientation, vocalization, and changes in sleep and wake cycles.

Urinary tract infections or puppy vaginitis may cause a sense of urgency and frequent urination. Parasites can cause diarrhea or constipation and vomiting. Sudden dietary changes or the addition of a new food or treat may trigger diarrhea and frequent soft, loose stool that moves more quickly through the digestive tract.

Bacteria, viruses, and inflammatory bowel disease (IBD) may also cause an urgent, frequent diarrhea. Females in estrus, usually first observed at 6 to 8 months of age, often urinate more frequently. Sexually mature male dogs, at 6 to 24 months old, may start exhibiting territorial marking behavior, usually on vertical surfaces. Neutering can help deter most of this behavior. Toxins, such as antifreeze, which have been ingested may cause vomiting, diarrhea, and urination. Hormonal or age-influenced incontinence may develop and cause urine leakage, especially when the dog is at rest. Some congenital diseases, such as bladder wall defects, also can cause more frequent, sporadic urination. Excess drinking (polydypsia) and resultant excess urination (polyuria) is a side effect of other medical conditions such as Cushing's disease or kidney dysfunction. Closely observe how often and how much your puppy is drinking and eliminating and for any signs of vomiting or dehydration. You can collect a urine or fecal sample for your veterinarian to evaluate. Arthritis, pain, cognitive dysfunction syndrome (CDS), or senility in older dogs can be a cause of house soiling. Separation anxiety often can cause a dog to eliminate when the owner is absent. Contact your veterinarian for an appointment to rule out any underlying condition that could be affecting the success of your puppy's housetraining.

Marking behavior is one of the biggest frustrations owners face and often is one of the most common behavioral problems that owners encounter. Marking territory is a natural pack behavior that signals to others their presence, sexual maturity, their territory, and dominance. At least 60 percent of male dogs will stop marking behavior within weeks to months after being neutered, and virtually all females will stop marking behavior after spaying, according to Dr. Nicholas Dodman of Tufts University. Neutering your pet also prevents roaming and causes less aggressive behavior. Spaying or neutering your dog is best done before age 6 months, when they reach sexual maturity. The longer you wait, the more likely the marking behavior will become a habit for your dog and more difficult to break.

Coprophagia, or the ingestion of feces, is a very disturbing behavior your dog may exhibit. It is hard to want to lavish those "puppy kisses" when your dog has just eaten fecal matter. Young dogs are more likely to engage in this behavior, especially when they are "testing" their environment with their mouths, but it can occur at any age. Dogs may eat their own or the feces of other dogs or other animals. Different theories exist as to why dog eat feces, and include exploring their environment, establishing intestinal microflora (beneficial bacteria and microbes), boredom, scent removal, or compensating for a nutritional deficiency. Mother dogs routinely eat the feces of their puppies up until 3 to 4 weeks of age until the puppy learns to eliminate outside the den space. The mother uses this defensive technique to maintain hygiene within the den but also to remove any odors that may attract predators. Rule out a nutritional or pancreatic deficiency and consider diet change to alter the stool. Provide your dog with adequate exercise and play to prevent boredom. You can apply an adverse "taste" to the feces by applying hot sauce or add a substance like FOR-BID™ (monosodium glutamate) to the food to make the taste of the feces aversive. Remote correction also may be used, such as the flag technique. Always try to pick up feces soon after it is deposited to keep your yard sanitary and to avoid temptation for your dog to find and eat the feces.

When frustration does occur, and it will, try to remember you are teaching a new skill, and it will not be automatic until your puppy practices it many times. When you find yourself overwhelmed with frustration or anger or wanting to become abusive, stop what you are doing, step away, take some deep breaths, give yourself or your puppy a "time out," give yourself some laughter, and freely give your forgiveness to your puppy.

CHAPTER **11**

Housetraining Other Pets

lthough the focus of this book is on housetraining dogs, many people will often want to know if their other pets may be housetrained reliably. Animals are inherently clean and do not choose to eat and sleep in the same areas they eliminate. With this underlying mantra as a guide, almost all animals may be trained to eliminate in designated areas. Cats, ferrets, rabbits, birds, and even mice, rats, and gerbils will eliminate in areas other than their eating or resting places.

Litter pans work well for cats, ferrets, and rabbits. They can be trained in a similar manner as described earlier for litter-pan training a dog. Obviously, the reward must be something valuable to the pet, such as a special species-appropriate treat. The litter substrate should be suitable for the species, and alternative litter substances, such as newspaper or pressed wood pellets, work well.

Cats may have certain preferences, such as clay versus clumping litter. Cats instinctually will bury their elimination and prefer to dig a small hole in a soft surface and then cover it immediately. Cats that are allowed outdoors, often prefer to eliminate outdoors in soft dirt, flower beds, gardens, or sandboxes. Many cats tend to "hold it" until they are able to relieve themselves outdoors. This is especially problematic for cats that are indoors more in the winter and do not spend as much time outside. This retention of urine or feces may cause urinary tract infections, constipation, or contribute to feline urinary tract disease (FLUTD). Obesity and improper diet may predispose these cats to the formation of crystals and urinary bladder or kidney stones, or even urinary blockage. A good rule of thumb for housetraining cats is to provide one litter box per cat plus one additional. If you have two cats, you should provide three litter boxes.

The box should be placed in a quiet area out of the way of noise or traffic. Your cat will not want to go to its litter box next to the rumbling washing machine or into the bathroom with the shower running. Cats will not want to eliminate in a place that they may feel is unsafe or that they may become trapped by the dog or another cat. Territorial issues may arise, and some cats may actually "guard" a litter box or stalk another cat as it is entering or leaving the box. This can be very stressful for a cat in this vulnerable position. Often, the owner will not notice these covert behaviors occurring in the aggressor and will not know why the other cat is eliminating inappropriately. Cats are territorial creatures, and inter-cat rivalries are common. Dominant male and female cats may mark territory within the house to announce their dominance over other cats or even the new baby. They tend to mark vertical surfaces, such as furniture, but also will seek out clothing, toys, or bedding. When a cat is stressed or ill, it may eliminate inappropriately outside the box, on your bedding, clothes, bathmat, towels, or laundry. It is often much more difficult to catch a cat "in the act," and therefore the perpetrator goes unidentified. You may avoid these problems by providing the appropriate number of litter boxes for your cat(s), choosing appropriate placement in the home, and determining if one cat is acting as an intimidator toward the other.

The type of litter box to choose can also influence the success of housetraining your cat. Some cats prefer open versus covered litter boxes because they will not feel trapped or have limited vision to the outside.

A disruption in household greatly affects a cat's mental state. For example, you have four cats that grew up together, were then separated into two households for a few years, and then rejoined again. This "new dynamic" might cause some cats to guard the food and litter boxes while intimidating and chasing the others. Cats are emotional creatures, and the problem might be resolved after adding more litter boxes upstairs and downstairs, establishing safety zones, and each cat re-establishing its place in the house. Geriatric or fearful cats may not, for example, be able or want to travel downstairs to use the box. Placing a litter box closer to them for easy access and safety should accommodate them.

Many owners face frustration as their cat prefers to use the dirt of their houseplants as the litter box. This can be avoided by placing aluminum foil, toothpicks, or rocks in the soil around the plant to make it undesirable to the cat. Cats are very fastidious about their cleanliness, and often will eliminate inappropriately if their litter boxes are soiled. You should be cleaning the boxes once or twice per day in multi-cat households and at least once every one to two days in a single-cat household. If you have ruled out a medical problem, behavior-modifying medications may be used to alter the cat's behavior. Pheromone diffusers (DAP) can be placed in rooms that emit an odor undetectable to humans. The diffuser releases a pheromone that mimics those of mother cats that may help calm and reduce anxiety in the household. These diffusers are available for cats and dogs.

Conclusion

lthough this is the end of the book, it is just the beginning to a trustworthy, healthy, happy house-trained companion. Your journey with your new dog will be a continual learning experience for you both. This relationship will continue to provide you with lots of adventure, discovery, and reward together with your companion. Just like a flower, as it grows and changes, it will show you all its color that makes it unique and beautiful, and it will enrich your life. There will be tests of your vigilance, perseverance, and patience, but you now have the tools to make the outcome a positive one. The guidelines in this book are just that — guidelines. Do not forget that your puppy may mature and learn a little slower or have a more stubborn personality that may alter the 14-day goal of this housetraining program, but the majority of them (and you) can learn it in two weeks. Do not worry if your puppy did not meet the timing goal — remember, all flowers blossom at their own time in their own color. A dog must repeat this newly learned behavior for about six weeks continuously before it becomes reliable and second nature.

You may encounter other problems or setbacks. Behavior such as submissive or fearful urination or defecation, territorial marking, forgetfulness or dementia, incontinence, or regression may occur. Many of these conditions can be treated with further training or medication. Other behavior training techniques are beyond the scope of this book, but this is where one of the most important aspects of training begins. Although this book specifically addresses housetraining, many other training tools are available through books, CDs, video, and professional dog trainers. There is much to learn beyond this first step, and all your further training efforts will be rewarded with a very special bond between you and your companion. Take with you the importance of the four P's, and you will be successful:

1) Perception

2) Persistence

3) Patience

4) Positivity

If you have decided that you want your dog to have freedom in your home while you are away or sleep with you in your room, you will be asking yourself "When will my dog be ready to graduate from the crate?" This really depends on your individual dog and breed. Most toy breed dogs are considered adults after a year, but many large breed dogs may take two to three years to reach adulthood. You can stop using the crate when your dog is completely and reliably 100 percent housetrained and never has accidents in the house. Your puppy is ready for unsupervised activity when he or she never chews or destroys anything except his or her own toys. You may start this process by leaving your dog alone for short periods, 10 minutes for example, then returning to check for damages. Slowly increase this period in minutes, then hours, to see if your dog is reliably housetrained. This could take a couple of weeks, If your dog has accidents, either destruction or elimination in the house, then go back to your crate training and gradually introduce non-supervision again.

Checklist of Key Points to Remember

As a friendly reminder and a summary of all the information we have discussed, here are some key points to remember:

1) Dogs are pack animals by nature and have the instinct to follow a leader. You are the leader.

2) Do not expect to completely housetrain your puppy before 16 weeks of age because they do not have the proper muscle development to be able to hold it for very long.

3) Be clear with yourself and family about the schedule and be consistent in your indoor or outdoor training methods.

4) Feed your dog a healthy, nutritious diet to help him or her eliminate waste on a regular basis.

5) Do not feed table scraps or treats in between meals during the housetraining period.

6) Until your dog is completely housetrained, confine him or her to the den space or crate, and supervise at all times when he or she is out of the den.

7) Follow your timetables and schedules vigilantly to quickly teach consistency.

8) Select one specific spot indoors (for paper training) or outside for elimination. This allows for scent motivation and easy clean up.

9) Take your puppy outside first thing in the morning, after every nap, after every feeding and drink of water, after play or excitement, and before bedtime.

10) Always observe and be alert for signs of whining, sniffing, restlessness or circling to cue you to take your dog outside for eliminating.

11) Always praise your dog after each time it eliminates in the correct area.

12) Use verbal praise and not treats when rewarding your puppy during housetraining.

13) Clean up any soiled areas, indoors or outdoors, immediately.

14) Keep your dog, crate, toys, and bedding clean.

15) Never physically abuse or punish your dog — the intention and tone in your voice is enough to correct your dog.

In "A Case History," in 2003, Anne Bobby wrote:

"There is no road map for a dog to follow into your heart. For some people, the road is just a little longer. But the road, once found, is endless and as rewarding as a raised paw, a wet nose, a kiss from the most loving of souls. A kind word passed unspoken from eyes that you can never look away from again. Nor do you want to."

Dogs show us loyalty, show us to be uninhibited in our emotion, and teach us the capacity to find joy in the simplest of things.

Congratulations on taking the first steps toward successfully housetraining your puppy and to a lifetime of new journeys together!

Other References for Housetraining and Behavior

There are many excellent reference materials on the subject of housetraining, obedience training, and canine health and behavior. Some good places to start include:

Online Information

1. **Pet Connection:** This website deals with anything to do with companion animals. Good Morning America's veterinarian Dr. Marty Becker and author Gina Spadafori

of *Dogs for Dummies* host it. There is also a blog of issues of animal care, as well as the Pet Connection archives, including housetraining basic points. Visit **www. petconnection.com**.

2. **Merck Veterinary Manual:** This online resource also is available in a great reference book form for a variety of species of animals. You can search a variety of symptoms and ailments or search a term for more information on the subject. There is also a detailed description of elimination problems with ways to solve them. Visit **www. merckvetmanual.com**.

3. **Association of Pet Dog Trainers (APDT):** This organization provides continuing education programs for dog trainers with emphasis on positive reinforcement and reward-based training. This website is geared toward professional trainers, but also lets the pet owner search for dog trainers in their area. The site contains articles, including housetraining issues, from the APDT newsletter, *Chronicle of the Dog*. Visit **www.apdt.com**.

4. **The Humane Society of the United States (HSUS)**: This vast site addresses animal welfare and advocacy issues as well as giving the pet owner good information on a variety of pet care topics including housetraining. House soiling is one of the major reasons that people surrender their dogs to animal shelters, and the topic of housetraining is of great concern to this organization. Visit **www.hsus.org**.

5. **Zero Odor®**: This is a product website guaranteed to eliminate pet odor. Dr. Nicholas Dodman of Tufts University, a veterinary behaviorist also endorses this product's effectiveness. The elimination of recent and residual odor is critical to the success of housetraining. This product will aid you in clean up and odor elimination. Visit **www.zopet.com**.

6. **Purina® secondnature® Housetraining Solution:** This website is maintained by Nestle-Purina and highlights its dog litter product. The site includes good basic information on housetraining, regardless of the product being used. Visit **www.doglitter.com**.

7. **UGODOG®:** This site offers the alternative to outdoor elimination training by featuring its indoor dog bathroom. It also contains good basic housetraining information. Visit **www.ugodog.net**.

8. **Cesar Millan's Official Website:** Founder of the Dog Psychology Center in Los Angeles, Cesar is a bestselling author and the star of his top-rated dog show, *The Dog Whisperer*. He offers educational seminars and provides training for unstable or problem behavior dogs. Visit **www.cesarsway.com**.

Books

These books provide the reader with more in-depth training information with techniques over a variety of additional training.

1. *Dogs for Dummies, 2nd Edition:* This book, written by Gina Spadafori, is an excellent all-around dog care book. It is a great reference for just about every question a dog owner may ask.

2. *The Holistic Dog Book: Canine Care for the 21st Century:* This book by Denise Flaim is an excellent reference for the explanation of holistic veterinary medicine available for dogs.

3. *The Power of Positive Dog Training:* Pat Miller is the author and renowned trainer of positive reinforcement. She easily explains the science behind positive reinforcement and offers a clear description of how to use these techniques to train your dog with wisdom and humane treatment.

4. *Puppies for Dummies, 2nd Edition:* Author Sarah Hodgson addresses all things related to puppies, including housetraining.

5. *How to Raise the Perfect Dog:* Author of the No. 1 New York Times bestseller *Cesar's Way*, and star of National Geographic channel show *The Dog Whisperer*, Cesar provides hope, awe, and aspiration for all dog owners to raise and enjoy the maximum dog companionship has to offer. He also deals with tough cases and deciphers canine behavior into understandable solutions for a variety of issues. His training information and programs are also available on DVD.

Magazines

Magazines, by nature of their frequent publication, provide up to date and cutting-edge technologies and techniques being used among us. Because canine behavioral science is always evolving and growing in its knowledge, magazines provide a more timely delivery of this information than books can.

Bibliography

Anderson, Teoti. *Quick & Easy Crate Training*. Neptune City, New Jersey: TFH Publications, 2005.

Kalstone, Shirlee. *How to Housebreak Your Dog in 7 Days*. New York: Bantam, 2004.

McCullough, Susan L. *Housetraining for Dummies, 2nd Edition*. Indianapolis, Indiana: Wiley Pub., 2009.

Millan, Cesar, and Melissa Jo Peltier. *How to Raise the Perfect Dog: through Puppyhood and beyond.* New York: Harmony, 2009.

Schwartz, Charlotte. *Puppy Training: Owners Week-by-week Training Guide.* Allenhurst, New Jersey: Kennel Club, 2003.

Verni, Lorni. *Everything You Need to Know about House Training Puppies & Adult Dogs.* Raleigh, North Carolina: Lulu, 2005.

Author Biography

D r. Gretchen Pearson has been practicing large and small animal medicine and surgery for 11 years. She has worked in a mixed-animal practice in Florida and designed and opened an AAHA-certified clinic at Elk Park Animal Hospital in Pagosa Springs, Colorado, where she practiced large and small animal medicine and surgery for 10 years. She currently owns, lives, and practices at Town & Country Animal Clinic in Park Rapids, Minnesota. She attended veterinary college in the West Indies at Ross University School of Veterinary Medicine.

Her interest in alternative medicine has allowed her to provide her clients with nutritional, herbal, and acupuncture therapies in addition to traditional medicine techniques. She is an avid reader and strives to educate herself on the most current therapy modalities available in the practice of veterinary medicine. She is certified in laser surgery and stem cell therapy. Her goal is to be able to offer her patients the most current and cutting-edge medicine and technologies for their long-term well-being, as well as alternative medicine and geriatric care.

She has served her community in providing discounted vaccination and spay and neuter programs and has served as vice president of the board of directors for her local Humane Society. As a volunteer, she performed prerace examinations on sled dogs running the 1,000 mile Iditarod race in Alaska in 2004. She also volunteers her service to injured wildlife and abuse and neglect cases. Her current animal family consists of two dogs, a cat, and a horse on her small ranch. She constantly strives to provide her patients and their owners with compassionate service and a lifetime of wellness in her practice of veterinary medicine and considers herself a lifelong student of the human-animal bond.

Index